"When is Daddy coming home?"

An American Family during World War II

Richard Haney

RICHARD CARLTON HANEY

Wisconsin Historical Society Press
Madison, Wisconsin

Published by the
Wisconsin Historical Society Press

Publications of the Wisconsin Historical Society Press are available at quantity
discounts for promotions, fund raising, and educational use. Write to the above
address for more information.

Printed in the United States of America
Designed by 2econd Shift Production Services

09 08 07 06 05   5 4 3 2 1

Library of Congress Cataloging-in-Publication Data

Haney, Richard Carlton.
  "When is Daddy coming home?" : an American family during World War II /
Richard Carlton Haney.
    p. cm.
  Includes bibliographical references and index.
  ISBN 0-87020-364-9 (alk. paper)
  1. Piddington, Vera Wolferman Haney, 1918–2003. 2. Haney, J. Clyde (Joseph
Clyde), 1912–1945. 3. Haney, Richard Carlton. 4. World War, 1939–1945—
United States. 5. World War, 1939–1945—Europe, Western. 6. Soldiers—United
States—Biography. 7. War widows—United States—Biography. 8. Children of
military personnel—United States—Biography. I. Title.
  D736.H364 2004
  973.917'092'2—dc22

                                                            2004008456

∞ The paper used in this publication meets the minimum requirements of the
American National Standard for Information Sciences—Permanence of Paper for
Printed Library Materials, ANSI Z39.48-1992.

"When is Daddy coming home?"

An American Family during World War II

Dedicated with all my love always to

My Father
J. Clyde Haney
1912–1945

My Mother
Vera [Wolferman] Haney Piddington
1918–2003

My Grandpa
Chauncey G. Wolferman
1894–1970

My Grandma
Mabel Wolferman
1893–1978

My Stepfather
P. A. Piddington
1911–1981

Contents

Preface

The arrival of the heart-breaking War Department telegram is planted deep in my memory, even though I was only four years old. The death of my father became a defining moment in the lives of both me and my mother. From then on, my mom and I forever were inseparable. The moment the telegram came equals in memory, and surpasses in emotion, the instants that I learned of the 2001 World Trade Center and Pentagon attacks and the 1963 assassination of President John Kennedy.

The writing of this book has been a labor of love for me. Among America's 183,000 World War II war orphans, I am among those fortunate enough to have strong memories of my father. And I am doubly blessed because my mother kept those memories alive by always talking about him. She kept all his wartime letters. It is those letters, her recollections, and my memories that I have used to construct this story. Her contribution to the substance of this book is immeasurable.

The story of my parents' and grandparents' lives during World War II is unique. But there are millions of equally unique family stories. My mother had always encouraged me to write about our family experiences during the war. Former Wisconsin Historical Society Press editor J. Kent Calder pointed out to me that my background as a professor of history with expertise in twentieth-century United States history, local Wisconsin history, and World War II military history make me a natural to write this book, and I am thankful that he suggested to me that I get on with it. I am indebted to the editors and staff of the Wisconsin Historical Society Press, for whom I have long possessed unflinching admiration and respect. State Historian Michael E. Stevens provided much-appreciated encouragement and suggestions. Kate Thompson has been invaluable to the extreme in her editorial, logistical, and substantive help. As a well-organized, observant, and upbeat editor who shepherded this book to final publication, she was the blessing that every author hopes for in an editor. Diane Drexler guided the book to conclusion by skillfully coordinating the numerous phases involved in making a manuscript into a book. My thanks as well to those who worked behind the scenes at WHS Press, and whose contributions to this book have been invaluable.

My gratitude to my mother and to the Wisconsin Historical Society Press for encouraging me to write my parents' story, and then helping to bring it to fruition in this book, is deep and personal. I completed the first draft in time to read it aloud to my mother, whose helpful suggestions enabled me to make several improvements only weeks before her unexpected death. That she heard the story of she and my dad as I reconstructed it was gratifying to me. That the story of my parents' lives during World War II has become a published book by the WHS Press is a dream come true.

"When is Daddy coming home?"

An American Family during World War II

ONE

Sparks at the Fuse Box

*M*y mother was preparing our supper late that afternoon, Friday, April 6, 1945, when two of her friends paid an unexpected visit. I was four years old. One visitor was Marcia Mills, who was the director of the pre-kindergarten school where Mom taught and which I attended. Marcia's daughter was an army nurse who had recently been liberated after three years as a Japanese prisoner of war in the Philippines. Mary Kamps, whose husband had died after World War I as a result of a German poison gas attack he had suffered while fighting in France, was executive director of the Rock County Red Cross.

Slipping her arm around my mom, Mary Kamps said that she had some bad news. My mother's instant thought was that perhaps my father, a combat soldier in the U.S. Army's 17th Airborne Division fighting in Europe, had lost an arm or leg or even his eyesight. In her mind, none of those things would matter. Then, Marcia Mills and Mary Kamps told her, "Clyde was called home. He was called to his heavenly home." Mom just broke down, covering her face with her apron.

I needed to know why my mother was crying, so to get her alone I insisted that she come with me to the bathroom. When I asked why she was crying, she told me, "Sometimes we have tears because we're happy. Sometimes we have tears because we're sad." She then said that although she was sad because my father was not coming home to us, we could be happy that he would be in his heavenly home.

Thirteen days had elapsed since my father's death on March 24. Everett "Pud" Harper, the Janesville Post Office special delivery messenger who assumed the heart-rending and burdensome job of delivering War and Navy Department telegrams to next-of-kin, was a personal friend of my dad. Two months earlier, he had handed my mom a telegram announcing that my dad had been wounded in the Battle of the Bulge. Harper was so devastated by the telegram announcing my dad's death that he called upon Marcia Mills and Mary Kamps for help. He had received the telegram early that morning, and many in Janesville knew of the contents by late afternoon. While Marcia Mills and Mary Kamps delivered the news to my mother, Pud Harper waited in his car on the street and wept.

After Mom telephoned her parents and Dad's mother, we went to supper with Marcia Mills and her husband, Charlie. Leaving house doors unlocked was not unusual in the 1940s, and by the time we returned, the living room was filled with flowers. Mom's parents, Chauncey and Mabel Wolferman, arrived from Madison soon afterward.

My dad, Joseph Clyde Haney (always called Clyde), was born on September 2, 1912, in Dakota, Minnesota. He was raised in Madison and Richland Center, Wisconsin, by his maternal grandparents, Ike, a cement mason, and Lydia Sharp. Dad described his step-grandfather, Ike, to whom he was very close, as "the only father I ever knew." They enjoyed going fishing together. His grandmother had become a strict Catholic convert upon her marriage to Ike Sharp, and Dad often served as an altar boy at St. James Catholic Church in Madison and St. Mary's

My dad, Clyde Haney, at five years old in 1917, dressed in his new Easter Sunday suit with his then-fashionable knickerbocker-style pants tucked into his high-top laced leather boots.

Catholic Church in Richland Center, where he received his first communion in 1924.

My father became self-sufficient at a young age. While he was attending Madison's Central High School, his grandparents returned to Richland Center because of Lydia's failing health. Dad remained in Madison for his senior year and stayed on after graduating in 1931. He worked at the Orpheum Theater on State Street to pay his rent and washed restaurant dishes for his meals. To earn pocket money, he delivered the *Milwaukee Journal*. Out of necessity, he learned to enjoy cooking his own meals. As a young man he liked to fish for bluegills and an occasional bass in Lake Wingra, hit golf balls at a local driving range, and play ping-pong. He was a devoted baseball, football, and basketball fan. His need to accept adult responsibilities at a young age developed in him a sense of inner security. It also gave him good judgment and a pragmatic perspective that enabled him to separate the important from the trivial.

Dad, shown here at about age ten in the early 1920s, adored his grandparents, Ike and Lydia Sharp, who raised him as their own in Madison and Richland Center. Dad made sure that his pet white kitten was included in the photograph.

My mother, Vera, was born to Chauncey and Mabel Wolferman on September 12, 1918, in the upstairs bedroom of their Madison home. Mom's parents had grown up on family farms near Black Earth and Mazomanie, west of Madison, and did much hard farm work in their youth. My grandparents moved to Madison in 1917 with a four-horse team pulling a wagon loaded with all their belongings. Throughout their lives, they held onto their rural roots. During World War I, my grandmother was required to appear before the draft board

My mom, Vera, at age two in 1920 with her parents, Chauncey and Mabel Wolferman. Mom so eagerly anticipated having this family portrait taken that she kept Grandma up much of the night before.

to prove her pregnancy a month before her baby (my mother, Vera) was born in September 1918, in order to keep my grandfather from being drafted into the army.

My grandfather was a paper chemist at the Forest Products Laboratory in Madison. His job provided stability, even during the Great Depression of the 1930s when so many others were unemployed. In his work at the Forest Products Lab, he had the opportunity to instruct visiting foreign paper chemists in how to conduct various tests. He often brought the chemists home for a meal, giving my mom, then a young child, the chance to meet professors and scientists from China, Finland, and New Zealand. When Secretary of Agriculture Henry A. Wallace visited the Lab in the 1930s, Grandpa described Mr. Wallace as being "twenty years ahead of his time" for his views on how to conserve and reduce waste in the use of wood products. One evening when Grandpa was working late in his office, the only other person in the building was Arthur Koehler. It was the same evening that Koehler completed the wood tests on the ladder that was the key evidence in the kidnapping of Charles and Anne Morrow Lindbergh's baby. Koehler ran down the corridor, shouting "Chauncey! Chauncey! Hauptmann's guilty! The wood matches!" My mother's father was literally the second person to know for certain who killed the Lindbergh baby.

Mom had an interesting and busy tomboy childhood swimming in Lake Mendota, riding her bicycle, and climbing favorite trees where she would sit and read library books. She attended Shorewood Hills Elementary School, where she was moved out of kindergarten and into first grade as a four-year-old who needed challenges to avoid what one teacher described as an inclination for "mischief." She attended the University of Wisconsin School of Creative Arts for Children for three summers beginning when she was seven years old. She won the Madison City Women's Doubles Tennis championship as a high school sophomore, graduated from Madison West High School in 1935 at sixteen years of age, and attended the University of Wisconsin.[1]

Mom and Grandpa and Grandma with their Model T car in the early 1920s in front of their home. When Mom was old enough Grandpa taught her to drive by practicing in Madison's downtown traffic. Grandma never drove a car.

By the time she entered the UW, Mom was an accomplished violinist and pianist who played first violin in the Madison Symphony Orchestra, the UW Symphony, and the Madison String Sinfonia. She spent many enjoyable hours in the UW's stately old Music Hall located at the bottom of Bascom Hill. She and her friends relaxed together at the Memorial Union overlooking Lake Mendota and at the soda fountain of the Rennebohm Pharmacy at the corner of University Avenue and Park Street. A degree in music was of little help to Mom in finding employment during the Great Depression, however. So, she simultaneously earned a degree from the UW business college and found work in the accounting department of Gisholt Machine Company of Madison and with the Madison Credit Rating Bureau, where she honed her uncanny ability to assess people's character.

My mom and dad met while she was attending the university and he was working as chief of service at the Orpheum Theater. One afternoon, Mom went to visit a girlfriend and her mother at their State Street apartment building, where my dad also lived. When the lights went out unexpectedly, everyone in the building gathered at the common fuse box in the hallway. When the lights came back on, Mom and Dad were introduced to each other at the fuse box! A few days later, they again crossed paths in the same hallway, and he asked her to go out with him the following Tuesday evening when he was off from work. She agreed, and then he told her that their first date would be a drive to Richland Center to visit his widowed grandfather. They were comfortable with each other and developed complete mutual trust, which my dad later described as "the most important ingredient in a marriage." Nearly two years later, they were married at Madison's Luther Memorial Church on University Avenue by Reverend Charles Puls.

Following their wedding, Dad worked for the Fox Entertainment Corporation in the Madison area. His duties included serving as an advertising executive and as an advance booking agent for live entertainment shows. He attracted numerous big-name entertainers to Madison for stage performances and built an extensive collection of 8" x 10" glossy photos autographed personally to him. His collection included Louis Armstrong, Benny Goodman, Duke Ellington, Jimmy Dorsey, Red Nichols, Fats Waller, the Ink Spots, Eddy Duchin, Bob Crosby, and Bunny Berrigan, among others. Scheduling live on-stage performances and promoting advance ticket sales were the easy parts of the job. With racial attitudes being what they were in the 1930s, my father also needed to make certain that he made hotel and restaurant reservations for performers such as Louis Armstrong, Duke Ellington, and the Ink Spots in upscale places where they would receive courteous and cordial welcomes.

A year after I was born (November 1940), my father took a job as southeastern Wisconsin's district manager of advertising and marketing for the Fox Entertainment Corporation of New York City. He was

Photo by F. Sanchez Gavieres, Madison, Wisconsin

Mom and Dad were married in early 1940. The photographer received a national portrait artist's award for this picture.

responsible for several theaters. To be more centrally located to his territory, he moved his family to Janesville, Wisconsin, in November 1941. He worked out of an office in Janesville's Jeffris Theater.

Janesville is located on the banks of the scenic Rock River, which had been the route of Sauk Chief Black Hawk during his return from Iowa to Wisconsin in the early 1830s on the eve of the Black Hawk

War. The city of Janesville was founded a few years later by settlers from New England and upstate New York. It was incorporated in 1853. Frontier aristocrat William Tallman, a perfume manufacturer, built an imposing brick mansion overlooking the Rock River in 1857 and hosted his good friend Abraham Lincoln as an overnight guest in 1859. Nearby church-sponsored colleges in Beloit and Milton were centers of abolitionist sentiment and underground railroad activism. Following the Civil War, the neighboring communities of Edgerton and Koshkonong built deserved reputations as leading tobacco producers. The first Wisconsin State Fair was held in Janesville in 1851, and in 1899 the Gideon Bible Society was born at the city's YMCA. In 1849 the Wisconsin School for the Blind, or School for the Visually Handicapped as it is now known, had begun a long and distinguished history of service to Wisconsin's visually impaired citizens and their families. Janesville remains the Rock County seat, and numerous sprawling and ornate Victorian homes were built around its courthouse in the decades straddling 1900. By 1941, more than two thousand acres of parklands dotted the city.

Janesville had experienced most of America's economic and social ups and downs of the preceding two decades. The General Motors plant had brought prosperity to the city during the automobile decade of the 1920s. The Great Depression hit Janesville harder than most cities, because new cars became unaffordable luxuries for most Americans. Labor-management strife compounded the situation. The plant ceased production for nearly a year and a half in the early 1930s. Annual local polio outbreaks reflected the nationwide problem. Janesville was even bedeviled by a rabies scare one year, when veterinarians and public health officials discovered that several dogs and rats were infected. Yet Janesville's greatest community trauma was still to come.

TWO

God Bless America

A Family and Community
Go to War

Shortly after noon on Sunday, December 7, 1941, Janesville's stately old Myers Theater on East Milwaukee Street was crowded to capacity for the showing of the hit movie *Shadow of the Thin Man,* starring William Powell and Myrna Loy. Movies had become a favorite nationwide pastime in the previous dozen years, in part because theaters were unique in having air conditioning. In the early 1940s, nationwide weekly movie attendance ranged between 85 million and 100 million.[1] The Myers Theater charged bargain Sunday prices of forty cents for adults and ten cents for children, plus the U.S. Defense Tax, which was already in place. As soon as the preview of coming attractions and the cartoon feature *Saddle Silly* finished on that Sunday afternoon in December, the Myers Theater projector was turned off, the curtain was drawn over the screen, and the house lights were turned on for an announcement.[2]

As Fox Entertainment Corporation's senior district employee, it fell to my father to have projectionist Joe Zigler stop the movie. My dad stood on the stage in the glare of the spotlight and announced over the microphone to the stunned crowd that Japanese aircraft had bombed the naval and air bases at Pearl Harbor in Hawaii and that the United States had entered World War II. Many in the audience had family members in the Janesville Army Reserve unit, Company A of the 192nd Tank Battalion, which was then stationed in the Philippines. My mom, who was also in the theater that afternoon, recalled that people were in a state of "total shock, mixed with anxiety for their loved ones and friends who were in Company A." Most audience members

Vera Wolferman Haney, about 1940.

left immediately, receiving full refunds for their theater tickets. For the handful who remained in the theater, the show continued.

Following the Japanese attack on Pearl Harbor, the war news became consistently bad for the United States. Japanese forces overran East Asia and the Pacific. The Japanese navy and air force controlled the western Pacific and posed a threat to Australia. The armies of Nazi Germany controlled most of Europe from the Atlantic to the suburbs of Moscow, their submarines were sinking more tonnage of American and Canadian cargo ships than we were replacing in our shipyards, and the conquest of England and Russia was not out of the question. Hours after the attack on Pearl Harbor, the Japanese launched a similar air assault on the American naval base at Subic Bay and the American air base at Clark Field in the Philippines. Japanese armies then invaded the Philippines, brutalized the city of Manila as they had Nanking, China, in the 1930s, and pushed courageous but overwhelmed American and Philippine forces onto the Bataan Peninsula and offshore Corregidor Island. The citizens of Janesville and the surrounding area were sick with worry for the local tank battalion men and army nurses.

Janesville was traumatized again when Bataan fell to the Japanese in April 1942. Following the surrender, the American and Philippine prisoners were subjected to the Bataan Death March, a forced march of more than fifty miles. Japanese brutalities against the prisoners were commonplace. Prisoners were denied water in the tropical summer heat. Japanese soldiers on trucks used their rifle butts to engage in batting practice on the heads of prisoners. Tanks flattened beyond recognition some prisoners who collapsed along the road. Hundreds of prisoners were executed by bayonet, gunshot, and machete beheading. Japanese troop discipline broke down completely. The world knew the Bataan Death March was occurring but was helpless to stop it.

Every radio in the Janesville community was constantly tuned to local station WCLO for any news of the ninety-nine Janesville soldiers and army nurses who were among the tens of thousands taken prisoner in the Philippines and subjected to the Bataan Death March. People bought every newspaper available to glean any tidbit of news about the fate of local men and women. The *Janesville Daily Gazette, Wisconsin State Journal, Milwaukee Journal, Beloit Daily News, Rockford (Illinois) Morning Star,* and other area papers sold out within minutes of hitting the newsstands. When the garrison staging the final holdout on Bataan and Corregidor surrendered, the Tank Company Auxiliary, composed of wives and parents of the men in the 192nd, met to read letters that they had earlier received from the loved ones whose fates were now unknown.[3]

Clyde Haney in 1942, before he entered the army.

Photo by Helgesen Studio, Janesville, Wisconsin

During the same month, as people in Janesville were brought together in a spirit of unity by the surrender of the 192nd Tank Battalion and the fall of Bataan, a local disaster compounded the community's sense of joint purpose. Helpless to assist the soldiers overseas, people joined together to battle the April 1942 fire that burned the Milwaukee Street Bridge, the main overpass spanning the Rock River in downtown Janesville.[4] The fire destroyed or damaged eight nearby buildings housing fifteen businesses. Eight fire departments, civil defense workers, Boy Scouts, and a pack of nearby bowling alley pin boys helped combat the blaze, and uniformed soldiers who had not yet shipped out helped the police direct traffic.[5]

By 1942, World War II had become a daily part of the lives of Janesville's 23,000 residents. Area citizens entered the military by the thousands. Janesville's "99," the men of Company A of the 192nd Tank

Battalion, were held in Japanese prisoner of war camps. Their families and friends had no way of knowing which of their loved ones had died on the Bataan Death March and which had survived only to endure captivity. War news dominated the front page of the *Janesville Gazette* every day, and much of it concerned local men who had been killed or wounded. Patriotic posters were commonplace around downtown Janesville, just as they were throughout the country. Mom recalled one, especially, in which Uncle Sam was pictured reminding people that "Loose Lips Sink Ships."

My parents lived what Mom later described as a "happy life in Janesville," where they made many good friends. She became the choir director at St. Peter's Lutheran Church, then located on the northwest corner of McKinley and Jackson Streets. Pastor Harrison Rex and his wife, Irene Rex, became a major source of emotional support for members of the wartime congregation. My mother and I made regular visits to the Janesville Public Library, on South Main Street on the east bank of the Rock River, to repeatedly check out my favorite children's books and records. I knew the shelf location of them all. Once a week, my parents and I ate dinner at the Chinese Chop Suey House on Janesville's West Milwaukee Street. My mother and father always enjoyed reading the newspaper together. Riding the Greyhound bus, or sometimes the train, from Janesville to Madison with Mom and Dad to visit my grandparents was always a treat. My father and my maternal grandfather, Chauncey Wolferman, had become good friends who enjoyed sitting and visiting with each other. They had the same subtle sense of humor and the same calm disposition. For a time, my dad's step-grandfather, who had raised him, lived with us in Janesville until his death in the summer of 1943.

During World War II, downtown Janesville was a thriving shopping and entertainment hub. The business district of Milwaukee Street ran for nearly a mile, intersected by the Rock River flowing through the heart of the city. The Monterey Hotel anchored West Milwaukee Street near the "five points" intersection, the Corn Exchange park, and the two railroad depots (Milwaukee Road and Northwestern). We lived within walking distance of the Milwaukee Street shopping district. In an era before supermarkets, Janesville was blessed with more than a dozen family-owned neighborhood grocery stores. The closest grocery

Dad and my Grandpa Wolferman, shown here sitting on the front steps of my parents' home in Janesville in June 1943, shared an interest in close family life and lively conversation and became good friends. They even had the same taste in shoes.

for Mom to walk to was Schoeberle's on West Milwaukee Street. Friends Joe and Dorothy Zigler lived on the Rock River, and to save on gasoline, Dorothy would make the mile-long trip to the grocery store in their small boat.

Janesville's many restaurants included the Chinese Chop Suey House, a family favorite. The Central Café, operated by Greek immigrant Jim Zanias, was located across West Milwaukee Street from the Corn Exchange. My dad visited Hack's Ice Cream Shop on his mid-afternoon work break to make his own malted milks every day. The Myers, Jeffris, Apollo, and Beverly Theaters provided entertainment in an era before television. (Through his job for Fox, my dad was responsible for the marketing, hiring, and managing of staff for all four Janesville theaters.) Emmit Doyle's Peoples' Drug Store, Helgesen Photo Studio, Bostwick's Clothing Store, the Resnick family–owned Elliott's Ladies' Shop, Gamble's Hardware, Rost's Furniture, Leath's Furniture, Cain-Ashcraft Furniture, the *Janesville Gazette,* and several barber and beauty shops dotted the downtown area. Tietz's Jewelry was next door to the Myers Theater, and Dube's Jewelry rooftop billboard dominated the downtown skyline. Harrison Chevrolet, Janesville Lincoln-Mercury, and the Dodge dealership were within sight of one another on Milwaukee Street. Westphal Electric, Woodman's Family

This was Mom's favorite photo of the three of us, taken in the summer of 1943 in front of Grandpa's car. Grandpa said that these happy smiles would make this picture a good advertisement for toothpaste. My parents were totally devoted to me and to each other.

Grocery, Gray's Bottling Company, the U.S. Post Office, and the Greyhound bus depot were nearby. The Rock County Courthouse, the Lincoln-Tallman House, Mercy Hospital, and a first-class public library added to the city's quality of life. Rock County Red Cross Executive Director Mary Kamps, Assistant Director Irma Mallum, and their staff were busy helping families who needed every imaginable kind of personal wartime assistance. WCLO radio had begun broadcasting in 1930 from its towers on Oakhill Avenue. Public and parochial schools, along with the Wisconsin School for the Blind, provided excellent education. Churches of a wide variety of denominations dotted the city. Palmer Park and Riverside Park provided scenic locales for family entertainment. During World War II, Milton Avenue was a blend of homes and farmland that in the postwar decades would become the site of the Janesville Mall and its surrounding entourage of businesses and homes.

My parents did not own an automobile. But we could walk most places we needed to go, and public transportation, in Janesville and throughout the country, was excellent. Intercity train and bus service was frequent. When gasoline rationing took effect, Janesville increased local bus service by adding routes and running on twenty-minute schedules. Special buses were operated for the night shift workers at

General Motors.[6] Janesville's several daily trains connected the community directly to Madison, Chicago, Minneapolis/St. Paul, Milwaukee, Beloit, Rockford, and Mineral Point. Uniformed soldiers, sailors, and airmen were always given priority seating, but civilians were seldom bumped on account of it.

Janesville filling stations had a rush of customers clamoring to fill their gas tanks on the final day before gasoline rationing took effect in December 1942. Gasoline A rations limited car owners to four gallons a week, later reduced to three gallons, and by March 1944 to only two gallons.[7] New cars were not manufactured for civilian use, and only used retreads were available to replace worn-out tires. Living in the shadow of Janesville's General Motors plant made no difference. The federal government decreed a nationwide thirty-five-mile-an-hour speed limit to conserve fuel. Whenever a driver was observed exceeding the speed limit, other motorists would often blow a Morse code "V" for victory (three shorts and a long) on their car horns as a reminder to slow down.

Wartime hardships were certainly a part of daily life. Nevertheless, in contrast with the depression years of the 1930s, the employment problem was one of worker shortages rather than massive unemployment. With the coming of the war, the depression generation had jobs in weapons and munitions plants. In the United States, unlike much of the rest of the world, people were secure from enemy bombs and the invading enemy armies that destroyed lives, homes, factories, highways, water systems, telephone lines, food supplies, railroad tracks, and everything else imaginable. My mother recalled that wartime life was plain and lacking in luxuries. But she remarked to me that because she "grew up in the Great Depression, the limits imposed by wartime rationing were not new to me, and I never felt deprived. I realized that I could not always have some things just because I wanted them."

Although Janesville and Beloit enjoyed huge wartime industry involvement with General Motors and Fairbanks-Morse, for example, the two cities did not experience the extreme social upheavals of Detroit and Los Angeles or, for that matter, Baraboo, Wisconsin. Janesville's auto manufacturing had made it a boom town in the 1920s, but during the Great Depression, new autos were an unaffordable luxury for most people. Because of this, Janesville's economy suffered mightily. The wartime populations of Janesville and Beloit remained much as they had been before the war, whereas many cities faced the sudden influx of large numbers of war workers from elsewhere. When the Badger Ordnance Works was constructed outside Baraboo, for example, that region faced severe housing shortages, school overcrowding, and other social dislocations that changed the community forever.

The University of Wisconsin, Whitewater State College, Beloit College, and the now-defunct Milton College were all located near Janesville. Home nursing courses were established to help fill the wartime civilian nursing void, which became an issue in Janesville when twenty-two nurses from the city's Mercy Hospital enlisted in the Army Nurses Corps. The curricula of home economics courses rapidly evolved from teaching how to bake bread to instructions on how to balance a checkbook, repair plumbing, and change a car tire. The University of Wisconsin began the Armed Forces Institute to enable wounded combat veterans to take correspondence courses while they recuperated in military hospitals throughout the United States. During the war, 403 University of Wisconsin students were killed in combat.[8]

The Whitewater campus lost twenty-seven former students in the war. Whitewater, where 1939 enrollment had been about one thousand, fell to a total of 339 students by 1944. Only twenty of the students were male. The football team ceased to exist. Homecoming 1943 featured a women's soccer game against Beloit College, but no wasteful bonfire. Gasoline rationing required that the basketball team, which reappeared in 1944–45 after a three-year absence, play only nearby opponents such as Beloit, Milton, and Carroll Colleges or industrial teams composed of workers from Parker Fuses or General Motors in Janesville.

Janesville industries retooled for war production. More women workers were hired. The General Motors plant in Janesville produced sixteen million artillery shell casings, mostly 105-mm howitzer rounds, by the end of the war. Parker Pen manufactured anti-aircraft shell fuses and radio parts.[9] Four days after Pearl Harbor, Parker Pen's Pen and Pencil Workers' Union Local 19593 voted to cancel its contract that dealt with overtime pay, hour restrictions, and premiums for night shifts. United Auto Workers Local 121 at the General Motors plant followed suit with a resolution urging factory conversion to weapons manufacturing and encouraging members to volunteer for home front war activities.[10] Rock County alone accounted for 40 percent of Wisconsin's sizeable number of government shipbuilding contracts.[11] Hough Shade manufactured blackout windows and curtains. Janesville Cotton Mills produced bandages. Rock River Woolen Mills made uniforms and uniform linings for the army and the marine corps. In Janesville alone, the total weekly payroll of industrial workers increased from $79,300 in 1938 to $144,000 by December 1944.[12]

Other Wisconsin industries rapidly converted to war production as well. Fairbanks-Morse in Beloit and Gisholt Machine Company in Madison produced machine tools for the military. Allis-Chalmers in West Allis manufactured bomber electrical systems and promoted its own corny version of Rosie the Riveter named "Allie Charmer." Ray-o-Vac Battery in Madison made leak-proof batteries, shell casings, and walkie-talkie field radios. The Badger Ordnance Works in Baraboo displaced more than 100,000 acres of farmland and more than one hundred family farms to begin manufacturing ammunition.[13] Oscar Mayer and Patrick Cudahy produced C rations along with canned and dehydrated food supplies for the military. Nash-Rambler in Kenosha manufactured military vehicles. The Manitowoc Shipyards produced twenty-eight submarines, which would go forth to sink 130 German and Japanese ships during World War II. The USDA Forest Products Laboratory in Madison, where my Grandpa Wolferman worked, did classified research on wood and paper products and developed improved shipping techniques for cargo vessels. During the war, my grandfather was assigned to numerous classified research projects. He was among the employees given top-secret security clearance, and he could not discuss his wartime research. After the war, his wartime work never became a matter of discussion, but he was always very proud of the United States Naval Ordnance Award pin that was presented to him around 1945.

To help integrate students at Janesville's Wisconsin School for the Blind into the life of the community, my father always made certain that the Fox Entertainment Corporation sponsored matinee showings at the Myers and Jeffris Theaters, without cost, for the students and faculty whenever a movie musical came to town. Movie musicals in the early 1940s were sound spectaculars, in part because nearly two decades had gone by since Hollywood had joined sound tracks to what had once been "silent" films.

Through his work for Fox, my dad raised more than half of the American Red Cross contributions for Rock County. He helped organize Janesville and Rock County war bond drives and March of Dimes campaigns as well. In one fund-raising event sponsored by the Fox Entertainment Corporation in 1943, Dad organized a tire drive by conducting a "rubber matinee" at Janesville's theaters. The price of admission to the "free" movie was the donation of an old tire to the rubber drive.

In 1943, Rock County residents bought a total of $7 million in war bonds during the Third War Loan Drive.[14] To raise money for Rock County's Third War Loan Drive, Dad brought the U.S. Army Band to Janesville and arranged a February 1943 Myers Theater showing of the movie *Yankee Doodle Dandy*. The price of admission in each instance was the purchase of a war bond. The Wisconsin War Finance Committee awarded my father a Certificate of Appreciation in October 1943 for his efforts to raise Third War Loan Drive money. For the Fourth War Loan Drive, Dad brought five decorated combat veterans to Janesville for an

Photo by Helgesen Studio, Janesville, for the Fox Theater Corporation

Janesville's Myers Theater marquee promoting the February 1943 war bond drive showing of *Yankee Doodle Dandy,* starring James Cagney and featuring George M. Cohan's popular and patriotic songs.

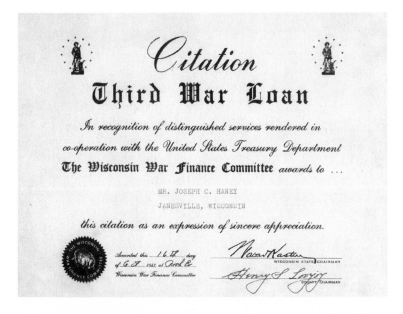

Citation

Third War Loan

In recognition of distinguished services rendered in co-operation with the United States Treasury Department

The Wisconsin War Finance Committee *awards to ...*

MR. JOSEPH C. HANEY

JANESVILLE, WISCONSIN

this citation as an expression of sincere appreciation.

Dad was proud of this certificate awarded to him for his success in war bond drive fund-raising in Rock County.

appearance. The March of Dimes War Activities Committee awarded him a 1944 fund-raising citation.

For another war bond drive, Dad drew a trio of Hollywood personalities to the stage of the Jeffris Theater on Janesville's West Milwaukee Street. The trio helped conduct a raffle of items that local merchants had contributed in exchange for an advertising plug. The entry price for the raffle was, of course, the purchase of a war bond. In the crowded theater that day, with movie stars on stage and my dad serving as master of ceremonies, I broke away from my mom and ran up the center aisle to the stage, repeatedly shouting "Daddy, Daddy!" As a three-year-old, I was unaware of it at the time, but the audience was so delighted that it is entirely possible I helped raise war bond money that afternoon just as effectively as did the contingent of movie stars.

By the end of World War II, Rock County citizens and corporations had invested nearly $55 million in war bonds. A comfortable annual wage was less than two thousand dollars at the time. The residents of Janesville alone purchased more than $20 million in war

Photo by Helgesen Studio, Janesville, for the Fox Theater Corporation

An eager, sellout crowd in front of Janesville's Jeffris Theater for a summer 1943 war bond drive. The lines stretched around the corner of the block in both directions. The Monterey Hotel is seen on the right. People dressed up to go to the movies in those days; note the number of women in high heels and men wearing shirts and ties.

bonds, which was approximately $875 (nearly half a year's wages) for every man, woman, and child in the city.[15]

United States government war bonds, along with federal income taxes (including a "victory tax" surcharge), helped finance the fighting of World War II. For individual citizens, bonds were a good investment. During the war years, people had jobs and income, in stark contrast to the Great Depression years. The demands of war, however, meant that major consumer items such as new cars, refrigerators, and houses were unavailable. Rationing limited the availability of meat, vegetables, gasoline, and other basics of life. People often had no choice but to save whatever money remained. By government design, war bonds paid attractive interest rates. So, for both patriotic and personal reasons, the American people saved what money they could by investing generously in war bonds. Newspaper advertising during the war routinely urged people to "Buy War Bonds," and one U.S. government poster encouraged Americans to buy war bonds—"the present with a future"—as Christmas gifts. Even Mickey Mouse, Donald Duck, and

Porky Pig joined the war effort when they promoted the sale of war bonds in theater cartoons.

Residents of the Janesville area, though, did much more than purchase war bonds. Indeed, the Janesville community developed a spirit of deeply felt support for the war effort beyond what might have been expected. The city agreed to tear up Janesville's trolley car rails along South Franklin Street and contribute them to war production. The Beloit city park's Civil War and World War I cannons were melted down to help fight World War II.[16] Janesville's Boy Scouts raised nearly a ton of old tires and scrap metal in a seven-day drive. Edgerton High School students gathered two tons of clothing and shoes for Russian relief. By 1943, Janesville residents had planted an estimated four thousand vegetable "victory gardens." Rock County's first seven draftees, all volunteers, were given a formal sendoff rally by the Janesville American Legion chapter. Throughout the war, Rock County Red Cross Director Mary Kamps and more than thirty women volunteers for the Red Cross Canteen Corps passed out coffee, donuts, and apples to every man departing for military service.[17]

However, local problems unrelated to the war did not place themselves on hold for the duration. In early 1942, Janesville's downtown parking meters became a controversial topic. The city had installed them with the intention of reassessing their value after six months. Over the objections of downtown merchants, the city decided to leave the parking meters in place to generate revenue. A year later, Municipal Judge Ernest Agnew dismissed a citizen's overtime parking ticket on the grounds that the parking meters were unconstitutional because they partially infringed upon the right of American citizens to travel freely. The judicial victory by merchants and citizens, however, lasted only until Circuit Judge Jesse Earle overruled Agnew's decision on appeal by the city council.[18]

In nearly every community, there was a handful of cheaters who did not know, or pretended they did not know, the answer to World War II's rhetorical question: "Don't you know there's a war on?" My father was quietly furious when he saw a stockpile of "black market" canned vegetables, purchased without ration stamps, in someone's attic. My mother's parents, my Grandpa and Grandma Wolferman, developed a lifetime of disrespect for a Madison neighbor who hoarded black market gasoline in an underground storage tank. A Janesville filling station was burglarized during the war by thieves who stole enough ration stamps to buy 1,800 gallons of gasoline.[19] Grocery stores were targets of break-ins by thieves who often stole a sufficient volume of cigarettes to either create a small invasion smoke screen or to start the thieves and their black-market customers well down the road to lung cancer. To eliminate theft, restaurants were forced to dispense rationed butter and sugar in small packets, abandoning forever the traditional practice of placing a bowl of sugar and a pound of butter on each table. In the minds of my parents and grandparents, the country's way of life hung in the balance. Soldiers were dying, and gasoline and vegetables were needed for the war effort. Most Americans felt the same way.

Mom recollected that she was particularly moved by Norman Rockwell's depictions, displayed on the covers of the *Saturday Evening Post,* of President Franklin Roosevelt's Four Freedoms: freedom of speech, freedom of religion, freedom from want, and freedom from fear. The Four Freedoms defined in human terms what the country was fighting for and reminded Americans why they were making their many sacrifices.

My memories of my dad and our few years together in Janesville are fortunately very vivid, a luxury sadly denied to many war orphans of World War II, Korea, and Vietnam. Despite my dad's full-time job and his fund-raising

Mom and I were forever thankful that Dad spent so much time with us and gave us so many fond memories. In the spring of 1943, we visited Cave of the Mounds, located between Mount Horeb and Barneveld, west of Madison.

I remember that my parents had such fun together and always made me so happy. It shows in the photos from our July 1943 fishing vacation to Pleasant Lake in central Wisconsin.

efforts, it was important and truly enjoyable to him to spend time with Mom and me, in no small part because he had been so very alone in the world until he and Mom were married. We were first in his life, and we both knew it. My dad spent a lot of time with me when I was little. He often "shaved" me in the morning with his electric shaver and once had me convinced that he had discovered a real whisker on my three-year-old chin.

For a week in July 1943, the three of us took a family fishing vacation to Sunset Point Resort cottage on Pleasant Lake near Westfield, Wisconsin. To get there, we rode the Greyhound bus from Janesville to Madison to Westfield, where the cottage owner picked us up in his car. I remember thinking that I was

I remember Dad telling me to give Mom a big smile while she took this picture of us on the pier at Pleasant Lake.

During our vacation to Pleasant Lake, I was excited to have my picture taken and to sit in the rowboat—even though I remained tethered to shore.

officially grown up when my mom and dad let me sit in the rowboat by myself to have my picture taken, even though the boat was anchored to the shore. Dad spent the week fishing in the boat out on the lake. A strong swimmer, Mom enjoyed swimming in the lake and relaxing on the pier. Except for one short fishing excursion with Dad in the rowboat, I spent most of my time ashore. He baited my hook with a worm, and after a few minutes with my line in the water, he excitedly announced that he thought I had caught a fish. The nonexistent fish "got away," but Dad had given me a good "fish story" to tell to Mom when we reached port! I remember that Mom kept a close and concerned watch on Dad, who was a poor swimmer. As a young boy he had nearly drowned, and from that moment on, he never liked to swim. For supper, Mom would cook the fish that Dad had caught and cleaned during the day. Our week at the lake was the only real vacation that my mom and dad were able to enjoy during their lives together. It was an idyllic and happy time.

At home, Dad and I often played catch in the yard or played with my farm animal toys on the living room floor or just sat and talked. When we played football in the yard, I was genuinely convinced that I could actually "tackle" my dad. Even though I had only a pre-schooler's concept of what football was all about, it was always a happy and fun occasion for me. I regularly rode my tricycle alongside him as he walked to the street corner on his way to the office. Just before Christmas 1943, when I was "helping" him decorate the Christmas tree, we knocked it over while we were "wrestling" but promptly reassured Mom that we would put it back up and restore it to good condition! It was his last Christmas at home.

THREE

"Well, Darlin', I'm in the Army Now!"

Training Camp

*M*y father was drafted into the U.S. Army in February 1944. Were it not for a number of unfortunate circumstances, he would not have been drafted at all. First, at thirty-one he was old to be a soldier. Second, as a pre–Pearl Harbor father he was in an exempt category until the Selective Service eliminated the 3-A classification for pre–Pearl Harbor fathers in October 1943. And two weeks after he received his draft notice, the Selective Service again stopped drafting this category. Additionally, my parents had mutually decided not to attract the attention that would have resulted if he had transferred his draft registration from Dane County, where he grew up, to Rock County, where he lived. That decision may have been their downfall. Individual draft boards possessed considerable powers of discretion in assigning classifications to individuals. Because of his fundraising for the Rock County Red Cross and his help in coordinating war bond drives in Rock County, it is not likely that the Rock County Draft Board would have drafted Dad into military service. But to the Dane County Draft Board, Clyde Haney was just another name on a list. As Mom later said, "They were scraping the bottom of the barrel at that time."[1] So he was drafted.

Dad was ordered to report to the railroad depot in Madison on a damp and chilly February morning at dawn. Mom accompanied him, while I remained with my grandparents at their Madison home. Several train cars full of draftees rode from Madison to Fort Sheridan, Illinois, near Chicago, where they were inducted into the army. From Fort Sheridan, Dad wrote to Mom:

Well, Darlin, I'm in the Army now. . . . We are only allowed
to wear fatigues. Had picture taken of whole gang that came
from Madison and Milwaukee. We are all in the same Barrack.
We sure look like a gang of convicts. . . . We have double-
decker bunks here (I grabbed a lower).[2]

During the week at Fort Sheridan, my dad experienced the usual
army induction routine. He received his service number, filled out
forms providing the army with his employment and educational back-
grounds, and took an intelligence test. Next came a brief physical
examination, fingerprinting, and a G.I. haircut. He learned how to
salute and to march in formation. He stood in a long line to receive
shots for a wide variety of horrible-sounding diseases. An anonymous
Fort Sheridan army sergeant even thought that he taught my father,
who had been self-sufficient as a youth and was a thirty-one-year-old
married family man, how to make a bunk bed. Finally came the army's
standard lectures to recruits on morals and on the articles of war. After
a week at Fort Sheridan's induction center, my dad learned how to
become a sardine by being packed into the back of an army truck for
the short ride to a Chicago-area railroad station. Truckloads of men
then boarded a train that would take them to a destination that the
army felt no need to disclose to the new soldiers until their arrival.

Dad rode a crowded troop train to distant Camp Blanding,
Florida, where he would endure a grueling seventeen weeks of basic
training. The train, of course, was powered by a big black coal-fed
steam engine. The trip took sixty hours because "they routed us crazy"
and "we could not even get off to stretch." Besides, he said, it was a
"funny feeling getting aboard a train and not knowing where you're
going. . . . I sure miss you and Butch" (his nickname for me).[3]

During World War II, most soldiers were moved throughout the
United States by railroad. My father was not unusual among Americans
at the time who had never traveled far from their homes. The Model T
cars and dirt roads of the 1920s were not conducive to lengthy travel,
and the depression of the 1930s made distant vacations an unaffordable
luxury for most. Before going to Florida for basic training, the farthest
Dad had been from south-central Wisconsin was to La Crosse,
Wisconsin, and Chicago, Illinois.

Camp Blanding was about forty miles south of Jacksonville, and light years removed from the Florida of tourist brochures. The base population of about 140,000 troops was nearly double the size of Rock County in 1944, and the camp covered an area of 123,000 acres. Camp Blanding was actually the fourth largest city in Florida, boasting its own hospital, fire and police departments, telephone and telegraph service, and railroad operation, along with two bowling alleys, seven indoor movie theaters, two outdoor theaters where according to the camp handbook the men would be "entertained under the fabulous Florida moon," and "the finest beach facilities for the teaching of swimming and for off-duty recreation of any Army post."[4] Judging from Dad's letters, soldiers in training had little if any free time to take advantage of what the handbook seemed to portray as summer resort recreational facilities.

Upon arriving at Camp Blanding, any uncertainty the new troops might have had as to the purpose of their training or the gravity of the situation quickly vanished. The camp handbook made the goals of training quite clear: "Our enemies are tough, cruel, and highly trained. Their defeat is essential before this world can become a decent place in which to live. . . . Learn your lessons well during your training period and avoid having your mistakes marked by a cross on the battle field."[5]

At Camp Blanding my dad was placed in an advanced Intelligence Reconnaissance unit. The officers, he said, were a nice bunch, but the sergeants were "tough as nails."[6] He was physically able to withstand the Intelligence Reconnaissance training, which was more rigorous and intense than that given to regular infantry units. The usual

Dad in spring 1944, wearing his dress khakis in front of the barracks at Camp Blanding, Florida. Mom sent the film to Dad for use in the camera that belonged to one of the other soldiers in the platoon.

seventeen weeks of physical training was crowded into the first six weeks, followed by nine weeks of advanced classroom work and finally two weeks on field maneuvers. Intelligence Reconnaissance training included learning to penetrate enemy lines, gather assigned information, and get the information back to headquarters. It involved practice in stringing telephone wires, reading and drawing terrain maps, and coordinating map grids. Because Dad was color blind, he had the advantage of being able to see through military camouflage. Recruits not only practiced how to drive jeeps and light trucks, but also learned how to mechanically maintain and repair them. By the end of the seventeen weeks, my dad was among the elite 60 to 70 percent who completed the Intelligence Reconnaissance training. The rest were weeded out and sent back to ordinary infantry rifle companies.[7]

Training camp was what the army intended it to be: a tiring and grueling regimen designed to prepare men for World War II combat against Nazi Germany and Imperial Japan. Camp Blanding was hot and humid in the summer, and the men's wool uniforms compounded that challenge. Even socks were woolen, because "they are the only ones that protect your feet against these heavy shoes." Wake-up was at 5:30 a.m. daily, bedtime at 9:30 p.m., and lights out at 11:00 p.m., until firing range exercises began at 4:30 a.m. with a six-mile speed-march to the range. Dad wrote to Mom that the saying around Camp Blanding was, "[F]rom 12 midnight until 4 in the morning is your own time."[8]

Physical training consisted initially of workouts, followed by double-timing while carrying packs and rifles. The men attended two-hour classes on two evenings each week. The next phase was learning to dig foxholes and belly crawl: "Boy is it ever tough to cradle that rifle so not to get dirt in it and pull yourself forward on your elbows with the rest of you flat on the ground." The rifle firing range, grenade and bazooka practice, and hand-to-hand combat were part of the routine. After dark one evening, Dad's training company went out to a large open field for a lesson in distinguishing various sounds at night. An exercise followed to demonstrate how easy it was to see people moving in the dark and how difficult it was to see people when they stood motionless.[9]

My father learned what every soldier is taught in basic training: Rifles are a soldier's best friend, and they will be cleaned every night. The rifle was a standard .30 caliber M-1 weighing about nine pounds, plus a one-pound bayonet and an ammunition belt carrying forty rounds. Dad commented that it was hard "to keep that rifle clean around here with all this sand. It takes about an hour to clean that every night and that's done on our own time." One grain of sand on a rifle during daily inspection got the offender placed on "special detail."[10] Surprise "breakdown" inspections required all men in the company to take every piece of their rifles apart, clean them, lay them out for inspection, and reassemble them. Once, when about half of Dad's company failed to have completely sand-free rifles, "they restricted the whole company to the barracks for a day." The sand was so prevalent at Camp Blanding that "you sink about three inches wherever you step." Less inviting than the sand, however, were the swamps, where the men were "supposed to get two or three days in before we leave. Coral snakes too."[11]

Dad dressed in his combat uniform, standing at attention with his M-1 rifle, in front of the Camp Blanding barracks during training camp. This pose was so out of character for him that he must have had a hard time to keep from laughing.

KP (kitchen police) duty and guard duty were added to every soldier's schedule at times throughout training camp. My dad wrote to my mom that

> Tuesday I was on K.P. and I started at 5:30 a.m. washing pots and pans all day until 9:15 p.m. . . . . I sat down three times all day—twice to eat and once for about one hour to peel potatoes. . . . Then on Wednesday I was a table waiter. . . . Then we cleaned all the tables and swept and scrubbed the floors . . . then at noon the same procedure . . . and at night we repeated everything.[12]

During monthly duty as Corporal of the Guard, his job was to take men to their guard posts, sleep in his clothes in the guardhouse, and be ready to assist the guard if any problem arose. During that duty he was excused from a turn at KP.[13]

Dad was clearly homesick throughout training camp. He wrote, "I sure miss the kitchen table and my honey's. How is Butch? Does he miss me? What questions does he ask and what do you tell him?" In another letter, he said, "I miss my boy. Are you being good to mommy?" My grandfather, Chauncey Wolferman, wrote to my dad that I had learned to sip soda "through a straw" for the first time. Dad told my mom to "Give Butch a bunch of hugs and kisses for me and tell him he's supposed to give you lots of them for me." He wondered if Mom had measured me on the kitchen door and how much taller I had grown "since daddy went to the Army." After being away for six weeks, he asked, "Does Butch still look and ask for me? I sure miss you both." Mail from home was clearly the highlight of the day at Camp Blanding.[14]

My father missed his family and would much rather have been home than in the army. But like everyone, he made the best of it. Nevertheless, as the weeks wore on at Camp Blanding, he was clearly not enamored with his army training. He wrote to Mom:

> Toots, this is the nuts. Yesterday morning we went out to a training area and had to start from a certain point by 4's and go through a wooded area and swamps using a compass and supposed to come out at a certain place one-and-a-half miles away. . . . Then last night we did the same thing in the dark. We never changed clothes from the morning and we were in water up to our thighs. Sopping wet . . . . Up this morning and the first hour was spent in hand to hand fighting. Throwing each other around.[15]

And my dad, who had never enjoyed picnics, said of eating in the field that when they were on the firing range or maneuvers, food was brought by truck and "we eat out of our mess kits. Just some more stuff to keep clean." On the occasions when food was not trucked to the field, the menu of the day consisted of C rations, and Dad remarked,

"I could not make up my mind to eat the stuff."[16] The C rations included canned meat compounds, including Spam, along with spaghetti and dehydrated eggs and potatoes. Although "C" did not stand for "cold" food, the description fit.

During basic training, my father was offered the opportunity to attend Officer Candidate School. Army officials saw a thirty-one-year-old with managerial and business experience who had hired and supervised employees for the Fox Entertainment Corporation, and they concluded that he would be an ideal officer. He declined, however, "because he did not want the responsibility of giving orders to twenty-five men and risking his neck every time he stuck his head out of a foxhole."[17] In retrospect, had he gone to Officer Candidate School, it would at the very least have delayed his being sent into overseas combat. Even more likely, as an officer he probably would have been stationed in the United States if the war was not over by the time he finished OCS.

The United States Army in World War II was more truly a cross-section of American society that it had been during World War I, the Civil War, or any previous conflict in the nation's history. In these earlier wars, a Wisconsin soldier would most likely have served with a military unit composed mostly of men from Wisconsin, Michigan, Minnesota, Illinois, and Iowa. In other words, they all would have come from the same general background. But early in World War II, there were several instances where soldiers from a single community, county, or even family were together in the same dangerous place at the same time. The Janesville 99, taken prisoner by the Japanese in the Philippines in early 1942, were classic examples. The armed forces therefore decided that, whenever possible, combat units of all sizes would comprise a broad cross-section of the country. So, starting about a year after the attack on Pearl Harbor, a Wisconsin soldier would be in a unit that probably included men from the Texas Hill Country, New York's Bronx, Kansas's wheat fields, the Mississippi Delta, Maine's coastline, California's beaches, Colorado's mountains, and just about every place in between.[18]

My dad made a few friends during training camp. The men who were married and around thirty years old gravitated together. In a letter to Mom, he described his three best buddies. Pleyte was a

Milwaukee attorney who worked as a legal investigator for the State of Wisconsin; Leighty was a newspaper editor in Alton, Illinois; and Rhodes was a draftsman. James Pleyte and Rhodes had children under six months, and Leighty was another pre–Pearl Harbor father.[19]

Even at Camp Blanding, there was an occasional respite from the training routine. Movies were shown on some evenings for soldiers who were not sufficiently exhausted to take the extra hours for sleep. Dad wrote, "I just got back from a show here at the camp. I saw Ginger Rogers in *Tender Comrade.*" At other times, he saw *Cover Girl* with Rita Hayworth, *Pin-Up Girl* with Betty Grable, *And the Angels Sing* starring Dorothy Lamour and Betty Hutton, and *Going My Way* with Bing Crosby.

One of the men in Dad's company managed to get a camera. Since the PX was out of film, Dad asked Mom to stop into Janesville's People's Drug Store and "quietly" ask pharmacist Emmet Doyle to sell her a couple rolls of film, which were in short supply. A few weeks later the film arrived, and the men were able to take a few snapshots to mail home to their families.[20]

After a month at Camp Blanding, my dad looked forward to getting a coveted twenty-four-hour Saturday pass to leave the base. He and three buddies went to Gainesville, about forty miles from camp. They preferred historic St. Augustine, but a five-hour waiting line for the bus prompted them to get their passes changed to Gainesville. En route, the bus brakes locked and the bus caught on fire. They didn't arrive in Gainesville until nearly midnight, when a gray-haired grandma at the Service Center spent a half hour on the phone to find rooms for them. After locating a restaurant for a sandwich, they went to bed. The next day, they looked over the University of Florida campus and waited three hours to catch the bus back to Camp Blanding. So, except for seeing a wild boar and a turpentine plantation from the bus window, "all our time was spent in trying to get a bus and in trying to find rooms. . . . [S]o if I have to go through that every time I'd almost prefer staying right in camp." Despite the inconveniences, my dad appreciated area civilians. He expressed sympathy for civilians who got stuck in small towns for up to three days because they got bumped by soldiers from standing-room-only buses.[21]

A month later, Dad got another Saturday pass to go to Jacksonville, Florida. He went to a couple of movies and to a USO that "was kind of crummy." Unable to find a room, he caught a bus back to Camp Blanding the same night. He remarked that although Jacksonville was a nice city, the merchants "really rook the boys all around here on prices."[22]

Two weeks of field maneuvers, or "bivouac" as it was called, culminated the seventeen-week training camp. By then, the troops were able to speed-march four miles in thirty-eight minutes carrying rifles and full field packs. Many soldiers, my father among them, had never developed a civilian-life appreciation for camping. They viewed living in the field for two weeks of bivouac as something considerably less than an enjoyable country outing. In advance of bivouac, my dad wisely began to stockpile chocolate bars to supplement the unattractive C rations that would be the only food available.[23]

One evening in the field, Dad wrote a letter to Mom and remarked, "It's getting awfully dark and I can hardly see to write and there are no lights out here (except moonlight but then I haven't got you here)." Less romantically, he revealed that it had been raining all day and they had been walking through a swamp, all the time hoping to avoid encounters with alligators or coral snakes. They were soaked. A steady diet of C rations had made everyone hungry. The men were required to remain in their wet camouflaged clothes and sleep in wet blankets. Except for four days of respite, it rained continuously every day of the two-week bivouac.[24]

Dad's friend James Pleyte ended up in the infirmary and was set back a few weeks in his training camp schedule. He was later shipped overseas, was wounded in France, and was shipped to a military hospital in England in time for Thanksgiving 1944. Beyond that, little else is known about his military service.[25]

Throughout training camp, my dad was concerned that he would be shipped to the South Pacific rather than to England or someplace in the United States. Troops from the preceding training cycle from Camp Blanding had been sent to the Pacific via Fort Ord, California. Assignment to combat in the Pacific involved the potential for encountering tropical disease, fighting in unaccustomed heat, and other dangers that Europe did not pose, and Dad's hometown of Janesville had more unpleasant associations with the Pacific war than with Europe because of the local people who had been taken prisoner on Bataan.

Additionally, troops shipped to Europe usually had a period of respite in England before entering combat on the continent. When he was appointed squad leader with the temporary rank of corporal, however, Dad thought that he might be held over at Camp Blanding to become a training camp instructor. He was hopeful that there would be truth in one training camp rumor that reported that pre–Pearl Harbor fathers and eighteen-year-olds would not be shipped overseas. He did know that only those who were to be shipped overseas would be given two-week furloughs to visit home. Troops to be stationed in the United States would have to wait six months before getting a furlough. When his orders from Camp Blanding gave him a two-week "delay-en-route" to visit home on his way to an undisclosed port of embarkation, Dad knew that he would be going overseas.[26]

FOUR

"Tell Butch I'm Coming Home"

The Army Calls It a "Delay-en-Route"

*A*fter field maneuvers, my father could think only of "getting on the railroad train for home." He wrote to Mom that he bought a T-shirt that said, "U.S. Army, Camp Blanding, Fla." and one just like it for me that said, "My Daddy's in the U.S. Army, Camp Blanding, Fla." He instructed Mom to "[t]ell Butch I'm coming home to see him and he is to say 'hello Daddy' real loud when he sees me get off the train." Four days later, on June 30, 1944, Mom received a telegram from Chicago at 7:14 a.m. stating: "Arriving Northwestern station 11:20 noon today. Love, Clyde." Mother and son were at the depot for the homecoming.[1]

After four days on the train from Florida to Wisconsin, Dad spent from June 30 until July 13 at home. The days were idyllic. My dad and I wore our "U.S. Army, Camp Blanding" look-alike T-shirts regularly. We played catch with a football. He visited the Peter Pan Pre-Kindergarten School where I was enrolled and Mom taught. Mom's parents visited from Madison. When Grandpa wondered aloud whether Dad could speed-march four miles in thirty minutes with a full pack, as he had done in training at Camp Blanding, Dad offered to do so while Grandpa followed in his car. Grandpa took his word for it! Within the constraints of food rationing, Mom fixed meals every day that were designed to please a soldier who had just been living on a bivouac diet of C rations. And we took several photographs during his two weeks at home.

My dad had arrived home on leave only twenty-four days after the June 6 D-Day invasion on the Normandy coast of France. When

Dad and I wore our look-alike "U.S. Army, Camp Blanding, Florida" T-shirts often during his thirteen-day delay-en-route in July 1944.

Janesville's WCLO radio had confirmed that the report of the D-Day landings was true, the station began broadcasting the news at 3:00 a.m., when it was midmorning on the beaches of France. The Janesville Fire Department blared its steam fire siren at 3:05 a.m. Soon thereafter, Trinity Episcopal Church began clanging its bells. The noise awakened much of Janesville, and most tuned in to WCLO radio to find out what on earth the commotion was about.[2] The much-anticipated allied invasion to liberate Europe had begun. Upon his return home three weeks later, my father was as hopeful as everyone else that the European war might end before any more soldiers would have to be sent overseas. It was not to be.

On July 13, Dad boarded a troop train at the Janesville Railroad Depot along Centerway near the "five points" intersection. I remember my dad, with his duffle bag that so intrigued me, saying goodbye at the station. The train left early in the morning, as I recall. Mom wore her Sunday best clothing to see Dad off. I remember distinctly that my dad's last words to me were that I should "take good care of Mommy while Daddy is away at the army." In looking back on that day, Mom said that when Dad left she was naturally concerned, but that never in her wildest imagination did she think that he would be killed and never again return to us. When the train arrived at the station for a very short loading stop, I remember Dad giving me a big hug and kiss, then giving a lengthy hug and kiss to Mom. Then, he boarded the train that would take him away for the final time.

I was so excited to have my dad home again and to be romping on the sidewalk with him that my toes curled skyward on this picture.

When my dad got on the train, he knew he would be going overseas, but he still did not know his destination. He wrote on July 15, while still on the train, that any reference to a nonexistent "Uncle Will" in future letters meant he was going to the East Coast en route to England, and if he referred to "Uncle Clyde" it would mean he was headed to the West Coast en route to the Pacific. Eleven days later, on July 26, he wrote, "I guess it looks like Uncle Will."[3]

After spending one week in a comfortable brick dormitory at Fort Meade, Maryland, my dad was moved to an undisclosed port of embarkation to sail for "somewhere in England." From Fort Meade, he sent a fifty-dollar money order to Mom. Neither his army pay nor his poker winnings would be of much value aboard ship. The next day, he announced that he had "made another investment with the fellows" and would be sending an additional fifty dollars—an amount he amended a few hours later to $125.[4]

Once Dad reached his port of embarkation "somewhere on the East Coast," it took what seemed to be an endless stream of troop trains to fill one ship for the Atlantic crossing. His letters took on a more serious tone. He encouraged Mom to "keep the old chin up and not cause yourself a lot of excessive and unnecessary worry. . . . Butch is our everything, dear,

The three of us had our last moments together at Janesville's Milwaukee Road railroad depot minutes before the troop train arrived, July 13, 1944. I am thankful that Mom and Dad took me along for this farewell.

take good care of him." He increased his paycheck allotment for Mom. Like all soldiers, my dad was unable to reveal even the slightest information regarding the ocean crossing, beyond saying that it was "uneventful."[5] The crossing took the standard time of about twelve days.

The ship was one of more than five thousand cargo-carrying Liberty Ships built in American shipyards during World War II. Industrialist and shipbuilder Henry J. Kaiser had developed a technique by which ship sections were constructed separately and pieced together with methods similar to the way cars were built on automobile assembly lines. The vessels, which could be built from start to finish in six weeks, were a vital component of the war effort. They carried the men and supplies across the world's oceans to fight and win the war.

For their first several days at sea, the men were not even told of their destination, although speculation and rumor aboard ship accurately forecast that they were bound for England. One consolation was that by the end of July 1944, the German submarine menace had become almost nonexistent, making the crossing less dangerous than it would have been earlier in the war. Nevertheless, shortly after leaving port, a voice on the ship's loudspeaker gave the troops instructions to follow in the event the ship was torpedoed by a submarine. No cigarettes or matches were permitted on deck at night. During nighttime hours, hatches and ports (windows and doors) were to be secured. Emergency stations were identified. Lifeboat drill instructions were spelled out.[6] Nothing could be thrown overboard because the smallest amount of floating debris might reveal to any enemy warships in the area the location or course of the convoy.

Those on deck were to wear life preservers that resembled two air pillows over a man's shoulders.[7]

On August 2, while still on board the ship, Dad wrote a V-mail letter to Mom in which he made references to sauerkraut, liver, and a swimming pool of "Dad's"—referring to Chauncey Wolferman, mom's father, who had never owned, never thought of owning, and couldn't afford a swimming pool. The messages, which signaled Liverpool (liver and pool) and Germany (sauerkraut), successfully slipped past the censor.[8]

My dad's Liberty Ship was double-loaded, meaning that there were at least two men for every available bunk bed. The army stripped the ships down to make use of every inch of space. To call conditions crowded would be an understatement. The men, along with their duffle bags and their equipment, lived in extremely close quarters. Soldiers slept in shifts in triple-decker and quadruple-decker bunks. They traded with one another, between the bunks and the floors, in twenty-four-hour shifts.[9] Hot water for washing was not available.[10]

During daylight hours, soldiers crowded the decks elbow-to-elbow, with no room to sit down. My dad was fascinated by a group of porpoises that followed the ship. Those who stood near the rails also glimpsed whales on occasion. Everyone on deck could watch the seagulls, which provided air cover in exchange for scavenger rights on both sides of the ocean. During the "uneventful" journey, the only reasonable expectations were two daily meals in the ship's mess and a

I remember thinking at the time what fun it would be to go on a train ride with my dad if only I could crawl into his duffel bag when my parents weren't looking. I recall sizing up the duffel bag both at home and at the train station for just that purpose.

bunk to sleep in every other night. The Atlantic crossing had my dad's stomach doing what he described in a shipboard V-mail as the "Jumpin' Jive" for the first couple of days on the ocean. Seasickness was common, and the crowded conditions only compounded the mens' stomach distress.[11]

To pass the time, the troops engaged in idle chitchat. They talked of the baseball pennant races and whether the two St. Louis teams—the National League's Cardinals and the American League's Browns—would make it an all–St. Louis World Series (which they eventually did that October). Men told about their hometowns and showed one another photographs of their families. Their minds were mostly on home, family, and all of the familiar routines of life that they were leaving behind. Several soldiers played poker. A few had brought their musical instruments with them and provided occasional entertainment. Some groups sang familiar songs to the accompaniment of guitars, banjos, or trumpets. Once the ship neared the British Isles, the soldiers' thoughts turned to curiosity about England. Because no alcohol was allowed aboard ship, they wondered when they would be able to get a cold beer.

As the ship entered St. George's Channel and the Irish Sea, those on deck were able to glimpse land for the first time. Some spotted the western outcropping of Wales, which they probably never knew was Pembrokeshire National Park. But they did admire its green hills and pastures, which were dotted occasionally with grazing sheep. A few hours later, the ship rounded Holyhead and turned eastward in the direction of the mouth of the Mersey River to dock at Liverpool. The wharfs and smoke-belching factories of wartime Liverpool were a stark contrast to the pastoral English countryside the troops had seen from shipboard.

Dad's ship docked at Liverpool on August 6, 1944. As the men started to file down the gangplanks, they received the routine and much-appreciated warm welcome to England.[12] On the docks, a British band, complete with bagpipes, played a variety of popular and patriotic songs ranging from "Scotland the Brave" to "Deep in the Heart of Texas." English Red Cross volunteers greeted them with tea, of course, and doughnuts. Trains awaited the soldiers to transport them to the scattered army bases to which they were assigned. Despite their uncertainly about what would come next, the American soldiers enjoyed being on solid ground again after nearly two weeks at sea aboard a cramped troop ship.

FIVE

"All My Love Always, Clyde, England, 12–25–1944"

Airborne Training

*F*our days after my father arrived in Liverpool on August 6, 1944, he heard the news about "no more pre–Pearl Harbor fathers going overseas. It seems as though I am always . . . too fast for those breaks to catch me." The day after his arrival, he wrote letters to both Mom and her parents informing them that a friend named "Mike" (meaning himself) was near Southampton. On August 15 he told Mom that he was in hilly country, and, although he did not own a car, he wrote on August 25 that "I can't make up my mind whether to sell the Plymouth or not." From these notes my mother was able to determine that Dad was somewhere near Plymouth, and not far from Southampton, in southwestern England. In fact, he was stationed at Camp Stapley, about fifty miles from Plymouth.[1]

The 17th Airborne Division patch was a golden-colored eagle's talon on a black field. The 17th Airborne was known as the "Thunder from Heaven" Division.

The military routinely censored mail from servicemen overseas during the war. Soldiers were not allowed to be specific about many aspects of their activities overseas. They could not reveal their locations beyond a generalized "somewhere in England," "somewhere in Europe," or "somewhere in the Pacific." Because soldiers wrote their name, rank, unit, and serial numbers for return addresses, they could not give any information in the contents of a letter that would be of

Photo by UHL-ROSS

Dad's army portrait was taken after he completed Intelligence Reconnaissance training in Florida, shortly before he went to England.

intelligence use should mail sacks fall into enemy hands. Whenever a soldier wrote anything that could cost lives in war, the censors either scissored or India-inked the sensitive information.

My parents developed their own code system that Dad was usually able to slip past the censors. They agreed that whenever he began a sentence by directly addressing "Vera," "Dad," or "Tell Dad," Mom should look to the first letter of every ensuing word for a message. Both my mom and my dad preferred to write letters on regular paper. Often, however, they used V-mail, which had been created to save space on military transport ships. A V-mail letter was written onto a form, microfilmed for shipment, and then photocopied in reduced size for delivery. Though somewhat inconvenient for the writer, it was a creative system and technologically advanced for the 1940s.

Upon his arrival in England, Dad was first stationed at Camp Stapley, near Southampton. He felt like he was starting all over again. Several men who had gone through training at Camp Blanding at the same time as Dad were there as well, but he was separated from his closest Camp Blanding buddies. The English money system was puzzling, and the chilly and damp autumn weather was not enjoyable.[2]

But my father liked England. It sure beat training camp in Florida. He described the countryside as being beautiful, hilly, neat, and clean, but he added, "I'm still very much in love with Wisconsin in the good old U.S.A." On a visit to London, he attended a movie and commented that even though tickets were expensive "the theatres are packed" with both British civilians and American servicemen. Food, he said, was "about the most reasonably priced commodity over here," but he expressed the hope that food quality was "better in normal times." The London Red Cross gave American soldiers on passes a bed to sleep in for only forty cents. Everything else, from transportation to beer, was expensive.[3]

Attending movies in English theaters had several added attractions for American soldiers. Prior to movie showings and during intermissions, packed theaters would be led in upbeat group singalongs to organ or piano accompaniment. Almost without exception, London theater-goers would include "There'll Be Blue Birds Over the White Cliffs of Dover" in their repertoire.[4] American G.I.s, whom the British often affectionately referred to as the children of "Uncle Spam," enthusiastically joined the singing.

Visits to London were second only to mail from home as a morale booster. My dad, who had never been farther from home than Chicago, Milwaukee, and La Crosse, exuberantly wrote of his first visit to London:

> I went to London Sunday. I enjoyed that more than anything I
> have seen in England as yet. . . . I saw London Bridge,
> Westminster Abbey, St. Paul's Cathedral, 10 Downing Street,
> Scotland Yard, Buckingham Palace, and Tower of London. Was
> inside of Westminster Abbey and St. Paul's Cathedral. . . .
> Westminster Abbey (where all of the Kings-Queens and impor-
> tant people of the Kingdom have been buried) was beautiful and
> immense. I saw where [former Prime Minister Neville]
> Chamberlain was buried there. St. Paul's Cathedral (second
> largest Cathedral in the world) was beautiful. Oh yes I also saw
> Big Ben and the Parliament. . . . I had a chop suey dinner.[5]

He also saw the ever-present black-and-white "S" air raid shelter signs
that had dotted the city ever since the Blitz of 1940–41. On many street
corners, there were sand buckets for use in extinguishing fires from
incendiary bombs. Makeshift repair work was in evidence on buildings
that had been bombed.

Despite liking England, my father was obviously homesick. He
constantly asked if "Butch has missed me a lot since I left again" and
"How much has he grown since I left?" He noticed from September
snapshots how much I had grown since he had been home in July and
wrote, "I noticed it when I got his pictures in the sailor suit. I was com-
paring him in those pictures with those that we took when I was home
on furlough and there was quite a difference just in that short time."
Dad remarked that he would be "glad when I get home so I can go and
come as I please and hear noises other than planes going overhead." To
my Grandpa Wolferman, he wrote, "[W]hen I get back we will catch
every fish in Lake Wingra." He wrote to Mom that in mid-October
1944, Armed Forces Radio "carried the Wisconsin–Ohio State football
game . . . last night and I listened to it. Even if we lost it sure sounded
swell and I was sorry we weren't sitting together in the stadium watching it." In response to one of Mom's letters to him, he wrote that
"Butch wants to know when I am coming home—I sure hope its
soon." Of an army camp Thanksgiving turkey dinner with all the trimmings, he commented, "It would have been much better had it been
Home Cooked. . . . Man what a glorious feeling. Well, they can't stop
me from dreaming." He learned that a Wisconsin acquaintance who

was a member of General George
Patton's Third Army was in a hospital "somewhere in England"
with a minor wound, but they
were never able to get together
despite helpful efforts by the Red
Cross.[6] When Dad learned that his
Camp Blanding friend Jim Pleyte
of Milwaukee was hospitalized in
England after being wounded in
combat, he tried without success
to contact him as well.

By the fall of 1944, England
had been at war for five years, and
the results were apparent.
Shortages were routine and
rationing was severe. Private car
owners were not permitted any
gasoline. The egg ration was never
more than three per month.
Wrapping paper was not available, and newspapers were limited

This picture was one of my dad's
favorite photos. Mom took it and
mailed it to him in August 1944, a
month after he left for England. Dad
carried this picture, and a few others,
with him until the day he was killed
six months later.

to eight pages. Oranges were reserved for children only. Factory workers labored up to ninety hours per week. Troop strength was supple-
mented by the Home Guard comprising those beyond military age.
The Women's Land Army helped ease the manpower shortage.
Civilians volunteered as Aircraft Spotters, Coast Watchers, and for the
Ambulance Service. For their safety, millions of young children, the
elderly, and the disabled had been moved from cities to the countryside
during the Blitz of 1940–41 so that they, at least, would not be among
the nearly 88,000 casualties. People used the natural shelter of the
London subway for bomb shelters, and many built dugouts in their
back yards. Along with many homes and businesses, Coventry
Cathedral and the Houses of Parliament had been reduced to rubble.
Thousands of children were eventually sent to the United States and
Canada and placed in the homes of loving strangers for the duration of
the war until they could safely return home.[7]

The hardships affected the troops as well as civilians. My dad attempted to buy a birthday present for my mom in a small village near Camp Stapley, but "everything is rationed," including clothing. It once took him three weeks to get a new tablet of writing paper after the American PX had run out. Eggs were a rarity, so the one time the mess hall served fresh hard-boiled eggs, it was a real treat. The fruitcakes, candy, brownies, fudge, and a sweater that Mom and her parents sent to him were welcome mail deliveries. By early December 1944, the families of 17th Airborne troops had mailed so much candy to them that many soldiers were eager to share some of it with candy-starved English children.[8]

Much to England's relief, America's "friendly invasion" began with the arrival of United States forces. People who lived in the vicinity of American bases welcomed the young men and did their best to make them feel at home. With the arrival of American soldiers, food was more readily available for British citizens. Many in southern England, however, had to give up their homes to American troops for housing and training facilities, and even "[o]ld parks were torn up to make way for Quonset Middletowns." By late summer 1944, more than a million Americans were in Britain. One English source called it the largest "mass migration which has made up the history of the United States. The New World was ferried back to the Old World" in a matter of a few months.[9] Thousands of American soldiers would return home after the war with English war brides. Among them was my mother's cousin, who married a young English woman while he was stationed in Great Britain.

In England, my father again turned down an army offer to attend Officer Candidate School. He realized that his training in Intelligence Reconnaissance and being a squad leader at Camp Blanding were helpful to him, but he said, "I'm going to use that knowledge to the best of my ability for my own protection." Troops were kept in shape by speed-marching, with full packs, up and down the rolling hills of southern England. They passed orchards of apple, pear, and plum trees. Dad commented that he had "never seen so many rabbits in my life as there are over here. You scare up two or three in every field you cross. . . . Did see a beautiful Red Fox the other day running across a field. One of the boys caught a ferret the other day." He even saw a "new-born calf today in a meadow so I'll have to write Butch all about it." The rigors were less than in basic training, the officers were less demanding, and on Sundays Dad could spend the day reading, writing letters, and sleeping. He cast his 1944 absentee ballot for president of the United States about two weeks in advance of election day.[10]

My father volunteered for training as a paratrooper in the hope of staying in England and out of combat a little longer, and because airborne troops were paid twenty-five dollars a month more than infantry. Dad wrote that he was "not so sure that I want to see Paris or Berlin. If it would mean getting home any sooner—ok—but that (getting home sooner) is paramount with me now." Like most American soldiers in England, he was coming to the realization that the dangerous road back home might have to go through Berlin. He was assigned to the 17th Airborne Division, 193rd Glider Infantry, Company B, which was stationed at Camp Chiseldon, near Oxford, Marlborough, and the River Kennet. London was about sixty-five miles to the east. The Avebury Stone Circles and the Tudor-style Lacock Abbey were in the area. Villages with the very English-sounding names of Chippenham and Wooton-Basset were nearby.

Dad continued to send messages to Mom in their secret code to let her know approximately where he was stationed. On September 9, he wrote to Mom's parents that a nonexistent friend named "Jack Kline" was a nonexistent "Salisbury's Route Man," revealing that Dad had traveled through Salisbury, England, en route from Camp Stapley to his new post at Camp Chiseldon. In late September, he conveyed that he was about thirty-five miles from Oxford, which was the distance between Oxford and Camp Chiseldon. In October he said, "That Plymouth would do about 50 miles at one time—but not anymore," indicating that he was no longer at Camp Stapley near Plymouth. In the same letter, he asked his wife, a nonsmoker, "Do you still smoke Marlboroughs?", revealing that he was near Marlborough, England. In November, he asked of mom's parents, the Wolfermans, "Is Ray Swindon in the service yet?" There was no such person as Ray Swindon in the family acquaintance, but there is a Swindon in the Oxford and Marlborough vicinity near Camp Chiseldon. And Dad indicated that he was sometimes about forty miles from Southampton, which placed him at Chilbolton Field, a Ninth Air Force fighter base where the

17th Airborne Division conducted occasional training missions and had held an inspection parade on November 15. The censors failed to catch any of his camouflaged messages.[11]

Camp Chiseldon was located at Ridgeway View, about two miles from the village of Chiseldon. The army camp had its own railroad stop on the Swindon-Chiseldon-Marlborough line, which has since been abandoned. Camp Chiseldon had been a World War I British army base. The nearby village of Chiseldon, with numerous thatched-roof homes and cottages, is located about six miles from Swindon, a small English industrial city where the Great Western Railway factory manufactured railroad steam engines.

The 17th Airborne Division had arrived in Great Britain in late August 1944. Major General William Miley, a 1918 West Point graduate, was the commanding officer. At Camp Chiseldon, the living conditions were the most comfortable my dad had experienced since entering the army, and movies were shown regularly in the gym.[12] Compared to the deprivations experienced by British civilians, the spartan weekly PX rations for American soldiers were luxurious: two D-bars (chocolate), two razor blades, seven packs of cigarettes, one can of fruit juice, and a sufficiency of soap and toothpaste.[13] Soldiers who were so inclined could watch a movie during the evening hours in Camp Chiseldon's commons room. Among the wartime classics that made their rounds to the base were *Casablanca, Mrs. Miniver, Stage Door Canteen, This Is the Army, For Whom the Bell Tolls, The White Cliffs of Dover, Bataan, Thirty Seconds over Tokyo, A Wing and a Prayer, Yankee Doodle Dandy,* and the biographical story of reporter Ernie Pyle entitled *G.I. Joe.* Prewar films such as *Gone with the Wind, Mr. Smith Goes to Washington,* and *The Wizard of Oz* added to the entertainment.

Airborne training was demanding. The men did nighttime field maneuvers on Marlborough Downs and the Salisbury Plain in preparation for combat. Dad went up for glider training rides about half a dozen times to become acclimated to the experience, and he described some of them as being "quite long and rough." When the 17th Airborne Division conducted an urban combat training problem at Southampton, he was stunned when he saw "a lot of damage . . . from the Blitz of 1940."[14] Fields in southern England were converted to parking lots containing miles upon miles of Sherman tanks and artillery guns. Warehouses full of medical supplies were much in evidence. Country roads were lined on both sides with ammunition storage bays, jeeps, and army trucks. Sections of fighter planes and attack bombers were stored in open fields near air bases for final assembly in England.

While Dad was in airborne training at Camp Chiseldon, the disastrous British-American offensive in the Arnhem, Holland, region began. He reassured Mom in a letter on September 18, 1944, that his 17th Airborne Division was safe in England and not involved in the Arnhem operation. Several days later, he indicated in coded references that he was about forty miles from Southampton and about thirty-five miles from Oxford.[15]

In the months my dad was in England, the Germans launched their V-1 and V-2 rockets against English cities. Of the V-1 pilotless planes, or "doodle-bugs" as the English called them, he remarked about the "great deal of damage from the bombings and the results of the Buzz Bombs" on London. During an October pass into London, he heard a V-1 alert sounded, "but the buzzer landed out in the country"—still, close enough that he was able to hear the explosion and see the flash in the sky. He heard "one of the V-2 rockets land in London" in November. The more than eight thousand V-1s wrecked more than one million English homes and killed more than five thousand people in just eighty days in the fall of 1944. Then, the V-2 rocket barrage over the winter months of 1944–45 killed nearly three thousand people and increased the percentage of English homes destroyed or damaged in the war to 33 percent. Most places in England had modified the long-standing blackout to a "dimout" by autumn 1944, but according to one of my dad's letters, "you still can't see anything after dark and just go stumbling along." London was still under a complete blackout, which forbade even a fragment of light from escaping through curtains and required that glass sky windows on factory roofs be painted black. As Dad described it, "there are no lights, so . . . you continually bump into people when you walk down the street. It's that dark."[16]

The damage to English homes was staggering. By the end of the war, 3.75 million homes had been damaged or destroyed, roughly two out of every seven. In London alone, nine out of ten homes had been damaged. Nationwide, about one million homes had been destroyed

beyond repair. About one in five schools throughout Great Britain had
been struck by bombs or V-1 or V-2 rockets. The British noted that
many of the London neighborhoods that had been hardest hit were in
the slums of the city's East End.[17]

The V-1 and V-2 assaults on London prompted one woman whose
home had been destroyed to remark in semi-jest that her husband was
"at the front, the dirty coward!" The loud engines of the V-1 pilotless
planes could be heard in flight, and the terror would begin when the
fuel ran out, the motors stopped, and the V-1 buzz bombs dropped to
the earth after several seconds of frightening silence. Explosions of the
V-2 rockets could be clearly heard fifteen miles from the point of
impact. The British government censored the specific location of V-2
explosions to avoid providing the Germans with free information concerning their accuracy, or lack thereof. The British public rapidly came
to understand that when press reports referred to "those exploding gas
mains," it was code for the V-2 rockets. Three thousand American
troops from the Corps of Engineers were assigned to build temporary
Quonset hut shelters for hundreds of Londoners whose homes were
destroyed by the rockets.[18] After a V-1 or V-2 attack, the most reassuring noise in the world was the sound of the "all clear," a steady two-
minute siren.[19]

My father was away from home for his September birthday, my
mom's September birthday, my November birthday, and Christmas. As
early as October 1944, he was already planning for Christmas 1945,
suggesting to Mom in a letter that an ideal gift for me would be an electric train we could play with together. During another visit to London,
Dad purchased Mom's Christmas present, a silver bracelet that he had
inscribed with the words "All My Love Always, Clyde, England, 12-25-
1944." He purchased it at Bentley and Company at 65 New Bond
Street, W. (Westminster section of London) and wrote on the inside
cover of the bracelet's box, "Best Wishes for my Darling: Next year it
comes in person yet. Love, C.H." He arranged to have it mailed to her
through the Red Cross. The bracelet's safe arrival was paramount in his
mind, and he repeatedly asked Mom about it, even after he entered
intense combat during the Battle of the Bulge.

By October, mail delivery to England was already being held up by
the rush of Christmas presents taking up valuable shipping space aboard

cargo vessels, which also had to carry troops and supplies. In early November, Dad asked in a letter if "they are decorating any of the stores or windows this year" for Christmas. The young soldier in the bunk next to my dad suffered a particular blow from the mail slowdown when he received word that his father had passed away, followed a few days later by a Christmas card written "To Our Boy" from his mom and dad.[20]

From England, my dad mailed some English coins to my mom to give to me, commenting in his letter that "maybe these English coins will encourage Richard to take an interest in a history lesson in school someday." (Little did he envision that I would earn my PhD in U.S. history and become a university history professor.) In a "Dear Butch" letter, he advised, "You'll have to help mommy like daddy does when he is home!!! When mommy gets ready to get the [Christmas] tree—you get right in her way and help her decorate it."[21]

A few weeks before Christmas 1944, American reporter Edward R. Murrow broadcast from London:

> At home we fought this war in the light. Such homes as we had we still have. Our whole industrial plant is undamaged by war. Our nerves have not been tested and twisted by bombs and doodlebugs . . . and things that arrive without warning. . . .
>
> There is a dim light in Europe now. The blackout is gradually lifting. And when I leave this studio tonight I shall walk up a street in which there is light, not much, but more than there has been for five and a half years. You come to know a street pretty well in that time—the holes in the wooden paving blocks where the incendiaries burnt themselves out, the synagogue . . . which has defied four winters. . . . It is a street where in '40 and '41 the fires made the raindrops on the window look like drops of blood on a mirror. It's an unimportant street where friends died.[22]

For Ed Murrow to see "a dim light in Europe now" was a reflection of the American public's guarded optimism that the end of the war might be near.

By the end of 1944, my father had been away for nearly eleven months except for a two-week visit home in July before he was shipped overseas. In that period, American, British, and Canadian armies had landed on the coast of France on D-Day and liberated much of western Europe from the Nazis. Allied Russian armies had swept through the countries of eastern Europe and were about to enter Germany. In the Pacific, American forces were liberating the Philippines and pushing the Japanese ever closer to their homeland. During that time, Dad had evolved from a civilian family man into a 17th Airborne Division soldier who had gone through both paratrooper and Intelligence Reconnaissance training. For my dad, whose life was hardly defined by the term "war hero," the early months of 1945 would find him immersed in combat that would result in his earning a Bronze Star for bravery, two Purple Hearts, one awarded posthumously and the other with an Oak Leaf Cluster, a World War II Victory Medal, and an Expert Rifleman's Badge with garland, the highest possible rating for soldiers. Those same months were a time of ongoing concern and anxiety for Mom, knowing that Dad was involved in intense European fighting with peace on the horizon. Even with the final victory in sight, the hardest and loneliest times for both Dad and Mom were yet to come.

SIX

"Maybe Daddy Will Be Home on Monday"

Keeping the Home Fires Burning

A constant question in my mind during the war years was why my dad was "taking so long at the army."[1] My mother wrote to my father in one letter, "This evening after supper [Richard] curled up in the rocking chair and said 'I want my Daddy—I want my Daddy.' He is getting impatient."[2] Another time, she wrote to him that four-year-old "Richard says that when you come home you have to get him a baseball, bat, and a baseball glove and then play baseball with him on the sidewalk. I asked him where Daddy was going to get all these things and he said 'Gambles [hardware store]—I saw some there.' "[3]

My parents were linked to each other by the chain of letters that the two of them wrote almost daily. Mom wrote a letter to Dad every night, seated at a small fumed oak table in the dining room. I would sit with her and write a "letter" composed of scribbles to my dad. Security and wartime mail delivery, of course, meant that the letters were sometimes held up for weeks and would arrive in bunches. I recall that after the mail carrier came, Mom would rush to the mailbox by our front door and usually find it either stuffed with several letters or completely empty.

Mom followed the war on the radio and in the newspapers. Movie theater newsreels provided the best source of visual war news in an era before television. She faithfully read Ernie Pyle's column in the *Janesville Gazette* and *Wisconsin State Journal.* Pyle was the syndicated columnist who lived with ordinary soldiers and wrote about their lives. On the radio she listened to Hans V. Kaltenborn's newscasts and Edward R. Murrow's live broadcasts from London. By piecing together

bits of news, she charted my dad's location on a large wall map near the
front door. In one letter, Mom wrote to him that

> Tonight Richard and I were talking . . . and I said that some-
> time we would go up to the Wisconsin Dells. . . . Then his little
> lip started to quiver and tears came to his eyes and he said
> "yes—but you take me up there . . . because Daddy is taking
> so long to come home." So I said we would go this summer.
> Then he said "maybe Daddy will be home on Monday." He
> really misses you and thinks you've been away long enough.[4]

Five days after my mother wrote that letter, my dad was killed in combat. The letter came back marked "Deceased—Return to Sender."

In addition to Mom's daily letters to Dad, she often mailed him
packages of cookies, candy, fruitcakes, and dried soups. Her parents did
the same. In order to receive mailings of candy from home, soldiers
were required by the government's war rationing board to make specific
written requests in their letters, and Dad cheerfully did so. While he
was in England, Mom and Grandpa and Grandma also sent him a
heavy wool sweater to help ward off the damp chill of English weather.

When my dad entered the army, his civilian-life salary from Fox
Entertainment Corporation was, of course, suspended for the duration
of the war. Family finances became tight, especially with a young child
to raise. Mom received ninety dollars a month from Dad's army pay, of
which nearly two-thirds went for housing expenses (forty dollars a
month); gas, electricity, and telephone costs (twelve dollars a month);
and milk (five dollars a month). Only thirty-three dollars remained to
buy everything else, including groceries. Mom supported us by working to supplement Dad's limited army pay allotment. She continued to
direct the St. Peter's Lutheran Church choir and gave weekly private
violin lessons in our home to twenty-seven pupils. (One of her young
students was always accompanied by his two sisters, who watched and
absorbed enough to gain what Mom always suspected was three lessons
for the price of one.) Mom's friend Marina Bliss took violin lessons
from her, mostly as a kindhearted excuse to provide financial help.

While my mom taught her violin students, I would usually play
quietly in the adjoining room. On occasion, I repaired to the kitchen

refrigerator to drink what seemed to be a fantastic midafternoon treat for my four-year-old taste buds—cod liver oil, unflavored and tasting like the fish oil it was, straight from the bottle. Mom's teenaged cousin Carolyn Peterson, on a visit from Black Earth, occupied my time during one violin lesson afternoon by taking me to the front porch and teaching me how to sing every verse of the popular song "Mairzy Doats." In addition to giving violin lessons, Mom took a job in the classified ad department of the *Janesville Gazette* for a short time. Later, she taught pre-kindergarten school.

With husbands, brothers, and fathers away fighting World War II, a generation of American women learned to become more independent than their mothers had been. Female assembly-line workers, a rarity before the war, were a routine wartime necessity to enable the United States to produce a sufficient volume of weapons and ammunition. My mother was much more independent than most women of her generation. She had been a professional musician, a corporate accountant, and among other skills could both drive a car and change its tires. Grandpa had taught her to be an accurate shot with a .22-caliber rifle when she was a young girl.

Mom did not own a car or bicycle during the war, so she always walked to the grocery store. Milk, however, was delivered door to door in wartime Janesville. The Pure Milk Company delivered milk with a horse-drawn wagon, which always fascinated the children along the route. Arbuthnot Dairy used a milk truck. To conserve glass for the war effort, customers were required to leave the empty glass milk bottles on their doorsteps in order for a new delivery request to be honored.

When our refrigerator broke down, Mom donated it to a Janesville scrap metal drive for use in building weapons and ammunition for the war effort. She was lucky to acquire an old icebox, because refrigerators were not manufactured for civilian use during World War II. After Mom had spent a few frustrating months trying to cool food in the icebox, her father was able to buy a used refrigerator in Madison. It cost ninety dollars, roughly a month's wages at the time.[5]

Routine childhood medical problems did not take a vacation just because fathers were in the army. Quarantine signs were placed on the front doors of homes where children had measles, chicken pox, mumps, whooping cough, and other communicable diseases. Before

the war was over, I had endured a grand slam of every imaginable quar-
antineable illness known to medical science. The public looked upon
the quarantine signs with widely varying degrees of seriousness. While
I was quarantined with chicken pox, Mom ran short of food but could
not leave home without me. So, she phoned her friend, Alice Freitag,
whose husband Sam was a Janesville doctor serving in an army hospital in France. Alice suggested that Mom borrow the car belonging to
another friend, Hazel Sorenson, and take me to nearby Beloit to go
grocery shopping where we were not known. She did.[6]

The dreaded polio virus provided the nation with a third enemy in
addition to Germany and Japan. An outbreak in the Milwaukee-
Waukesha area resulted in the cancellation of the 1944 Janesville-
Waukesha high school football game. In 1945, polio took the lives of
sixteen children in Rockford, Illinois, which was only a few miles from
Janesville. In an effort to deter the further spread of polio cases in
Rockford, a B-17 Flying Fortress bomber sprayed DDT over that city.[7]

Starting shortly after Dad left for military service, my mother started
teaching at the Peter Pan Pre-Kindergarten School, owned and operated
by Marcia Mills and located in the Mills's stately brick home at 209
Atwood Avenue on the hill behind the Rock County Courthouse. The
social lives of many Janesville citizens revolved around wartime challenges
that people had in common. About a dozen of the mothers with children
at Marcia Mills's pre-kindergarten school had husbands in the military.
John and Priscilla Freitag's father, Sam Freitag, was an army doctor in
Europe. Carol Sorenson's father, Ted Sorenson, was a Janesville High
School coach serving in the navy in the Pacific. Donald Bliss's father, army
chaplain Donald Bliss, was stationed in Italy, and his mother, Marina, had
been a Russian émigré to the United States in the late 1930s. Wendy
Weiss's father, former University of Wisconsin all-American fullback
Howard Weiss, was a navy ensign in the Pacific. Judy Bloomfield's father,
Kenneth Bloomfield, died on the Bataan Death March in the Philippines.
John Rothe's father, John Sr., was a navy athletic director in Minneapolis.
Mollie Ehrlinger's father was terminally ill.[8]

The school became a social center for the children, and many of
the mothers became close friends. On warm days, my mom and some
of the other mothers would convoy the cars of Hazel Sorenson (a light
green 1940 Chevrolet), Marina Bliss (a bright yellow convertible), Ellie

This photo of several of the gang at pre-kindergarten school was featured in the *Janesville Gazette* on February 6, 1945, when owner and teacher Marcia Mills, upper right, learned that her daughter Lieutenant Marcia Gates, an army nurse, had been liberated after three years as a prisoner of war of the Japanese in the Philippines. I am in the front row, third from the right. Mom assisted Marcia Mills at the school and was a close friend to several of the other moms. Front row, from left, are Janet Morris, Wendy Weiss, Judy Bloomfield, Richard Haney, Sarah Lee Mitchell, and Bobby Allen. Top row, from left, are George Grimm, Dorothy Carr, Molly Ehrlinger, Priscilla and John Freitag, Donald Bliss, and John Roethe.

Ehrlinger, and Alice Freitag to drive the children to Palmer Park or Riverside Park to swim in the wading pools as a diversion from the daily school routine.[9] The group of mothers would occasionally go out to eat together, and some of them would attend concerts and plays at the Janesville High School auditorium on the banks of the Rock River. The wives and mothers of the Janesville 99, who were now prisoners of war of the Japanese, organized a formal auxiliary. Women who worked on assembly lines at General Motors, Fairbanks-Morse, Parker Pen, and other plants developed common interests. Others volunteered for the Red Cross Canteen Corps.

Janesville was fortunate to have Marcia Mills's licensed Peter Pan Pre-Kindergarten School. Nationwide, the war created a serious labor shortage and a glaring scarcity of satisfactory, let alone licensed, day care schools. Working mothers whose husbands were in the military needed a place where their preschool children would be safely supervised. Marcia Mills provided for Janesville what was noticeably lacking in many communities throughout the United States.

Janesville's excellent wartime public transportation system made it easy for people to ride the bus or take a taxi to save on fuel. In addition to being practical, it was also enjoyable. To cool off on hot summer evenings before home air conditioning existed, my mother and I would often ride the Janesville city bus around the entire line. The price of a city bus ticket was ten cents, and the breeze through the windows was refreshing. Because we had no car, we took a taxi to pre-kindergarten school for Mom's work and my "education" every day.

When my Grandpa and Grandma Wolferman could save enough gasoline rationing coupons, they would drive their car from Madison for a visit. They always brought a basketful of food, including Grandma's home-baked dinner rolls. Sometimes, we would eat out together at Tibbie's Restaurant at Indianford near Edgerton or at Jim Zanias's Central

Café in downtown Janesville. My parents and grandparents were products of the depression years, and they expected me to eat everything on my plate. I loved eating fish, but not french fries. So to get me to eat my french fries, Mom and Grandpa and Grandma once convinced me that French fries really were little fish. Suddenly, I came to relish those "fish."

To purchase meat and vegetables, among other commodities, consumers needed both

I spent much of my daily "yard-time" at Marcia Mills's pre-kindergarten school in that wagon with my three buddies, from left, Nancy Hartman, Judy Bloomfield, and Wendy Weiss.

I know that Grandpa and Grandma were terribly concerned about me and Mom and Dad after he left for England. We spent a lot of time together in the months he was overseas. For this October 1944 photo, Grandma and I sat on the running board of their car. In the background is the home on the last farm owned by Grandpa's parents, Ed and Beda Wolferman, a mile east of Mazomanie, Wisconsin.

money and ration stamps. The government's monthly issue of ration stamps consisted of forty-eight blue points for canned goods and sixty-four red points for perishables. The ration coupon price of any given item regularly fluctuated, along with the cash price. Because of occasional shortages, many mom-and-pop grocers would reserve cuts of meat and fresh vegetables for regular customers who had a family member in military service. The customers still needed to produce both ration stamps and money, but at least they would always have enough food. After my father entered the army, my mother was among those who benefited from Schoeberle's grocery store's adoption of the policy.[10]

Mom recalled that there was a scarcity of some food supplies during the war. By early 1945, bananas were difficult to find and ice cream was what she called "practically a thing of the past." She wrote to my father in March that canned vegetables such as peas were "so very expensive in the stores and the blue points they take are terrific."[11] By early August 1945, Janesville even experienced a brief shortage of toilet paper!¹² Shortages did not stop there. *Yank: The Army Weekly* news magazine, reported to soldiers that

> . . . you can't buy very much around the U.S. Try and find a washing machine, radio, phonograph record, electric iron or toaster, or a thousand and one things that used to lie around every home. . . . People who own vacuum cleaners are hoarding them. . . . And they are wearing out, too.¹³

Many Americans found ingenious and legal ways to supplement their food supplies despite rationing. Victory gardens full of home-grown vegetables were the most obvious solution. Many people went deer and squirrel hunting to put food on the table. Others went fishing in southern Wisconsin's numerous rivers and lakes. Mom's father expanded the size of the vegetable garden that he had always cultivated as an outgrowth of having grown up on his parents' farm. During the war, Grandpa also devoted several hours of his spare time each month to doing all the bookkeeping and accounting work for a lifelong friend who operated a small family-run creamery. In exchange, Grandpa received butter for his family's personal use. By law, no ration stamps were required for such a small-scale personal barter exchange.

Because of meat rationing, it was not unusual for Americans to raise their own rabbits, chickens, and occasionally even dogs to supplement their diets. Mom had purchased a dozen chicks at Easter, but instead of cleaning and eating them she gave them to an area farmer once they outgrew their cardboard box. The citywide animal population became a serious enough problem, however, that the Janesville City Council debated a proposed local ordinance to limit households within the city limits to a maximum of twenty animals, a figure that was to include no more than two dogs at a time. The council deferred action due to vocal objections by those citizens desiring to guarantee themselves an adequate supply of alternative protein! Nevertheless, the concerns of public health officials and of the city council did not disappear.¹⁴

Mom and I frequently rode the train or the Greyhound bus from Janesville to Madison to visit my grandparents. The two bus routes took us through Stoughton and Edgerton on Highway 51 or through Evansville and Oregon on Highway 14. During one of our frequent visits, the four of us used some saved-up gasoline ration stamps to drive to Baraboo to see what Mom described at the time as the "immense" Badger Ordnance Works, where Grandma's brother worked as a welder during the war.[15]

World War II constantly intruded upon the lives of people in Janesville and the surrounding area. Janesville had a large kiosk about thirty feet across on the

I was very close to my Grandpa and Grandma Wolferman from the time I was a toddler and am fortunate to have had them in my life until I was in my thirties.

southeast corner of the Rock County Courthouse grounds, at the corner of South Main and East Court Streets. The kiosk contained an honor roll listing the name of every one of the more than 2,500 county citizens, including nearly 150 women, who were in military service. A gold star was beside the name of each of those who had been killed. The list kept getting longer and the gold stars began to multiply as the war went on. After my father entered the service, Mom and I regularly crossed Main Street from the public library to view his name, and eventually the gold star beside it, on the kiosk.

The names of soldiers and sailors from the area became household words throughout Rock County. Dad remarked in response to one of Mom's letters that he "was sure sorry to hear about Billy Rost," the son of Janesville merchants who was killed in combat. Rost, he said, "was a good boy and its too bad."[16] Mom's next-door neighbor's son, Gene McDonald, was wounded when a shell landed near him and mangled his right arm and leg and caused lung bleeding from the impact of the blast.[17] Wayne Hyde, the son of my parents' dear friends Doc and Lydia Hyde, was severely wounded and was placed in a body cast in a Paris hospital to be shipped to the United States. It was common from D-Day until the end of the war in Europe for severely wounded

This kiosk on Janesville's Rock County Courthouse grounds listed all the county men and women in uniform, with gold stars beside the names of those killed in combat. Seeing the lengthy list of names from a single county helped bring home the enormity of the country's sacrifice during World War II.

soldiers to simply be placed in body casts by overburdened medical facilities near the front and shipped to hospitals on the East Coast of the United States to be treated for injuries. Even Janesville's Dr. Sam Freitag was sent home to be with his family for an extended rest. A urologist by training, his job in an army hospital in France was to spend seven days a week sawing arms and legs off wounded soldiers. Mom said that Dr. Sam had become "very thin and worn" by the time he got home. Near the end of the war, Beloit rabbi A. L. Rosenblum learned that both of his parents, his three sisters, and his two brothers had all died in the murder factories of the Nazi holocaust.[18]

In March 1945, Sergeant Dale Lawton, one of the Janesville 99 who had survived the Bataan Death March and been a prisoner of war of the Japanese for three years, arrived home to reveal the sad news that at least fifty of the original ninety-nine men of Janesville's Company A Tank Battalion were dead. His revelation increased by thirty-one the number of members of Company A who had already been confirmed killed. Until Lawton's return, Janesville area residents, particularly the women of the 192nd Tank Battalion Auxiliary, had been hopeful that

most of the men would eventually return home. Lawton's knowledge
cast a dark shadow over his own happy homecoming.[19] By the end of
the war, sixty-four of the Janesville 99 had died in captivity or on the
Death March. Only thirty-five survived.[20]

Lieutenant Marcia Gates, the daughter of pre-kindergarten school
operator Marcia Mills, was among the army nurses who had been trapped
with American troops on the Bataan Peninsula in the Philippines. Marcia
Gates had arrived in the Philippines in October 1941 as part of a contingent of sixty-six army nurses. After the surrender on Bataan in early 1942,
she was with the troops who took refuge in the Malinta Tunnel on the
island of Corregidor. Following the surrender, the Japanese were unsure
whether the nurses were military or civilian and so placed the sixty-six
army and eleven navy nurses in the Santo Tomas Internment Camp in
Manila along with 3,700 other POWs.[21] There they were subject to disease and torture and were placed on a slow starvation diet. Meals consisted
of pest-infested oatmeal. They were separated from the male soldiers and
hence unable to give them medical care.[22] General Douglas MacArthur
recorded in his memoirs:

> With every step that our soldiers took toward Santo Tomas,
> Bilibid, Cabanatuan, and Los Banos, where these prisoners
> were held, the Japanese soldiers guarding them had become
> more and more sadistic. I knew that many of these half-
> starved and ill-treated people would die unless we rescued
> them promptly. The thought of their destruction with deliver-
> ance so near was deeply repellent to me.[23]

Marcia Gates and the other prisoners at Santo Tomas were liberated
on February 4, 1945, after nearly three years of captivity.[24] When General
Douglas MacArthur first arrived at Santo Tomas, he recalled that:

> . . . the pitiful, half-starved inmates broke out in excited yells.
> I entered the building and was immediately pressed back
> against the wall by thousands of emotionally charged people.
> In their ragged, filthy clothes, with tears streaming down their
> faces, they seemed to be using their last strength to fight their
> way close enough to grasp my hand. . . . It was a wonderful

and never-to-be-forgotten moment—to be a life-saver, not a life-taker.[25]

Were it not for MacArthur's earlier insistence upon liberating the Philippines as a major strategic military objective, most of the POWs held there would not have survived to the end of the war. Many in the United States high command wanted to bypass the island nation and isolate the Japanese occupying forces. Fortunately for the prisoners, MacArthur's views prevailed.

During Marcia Gates's three years as a prisoner of war, she underwent surgery for cancer.[26] The conditions under which the surgery took place can only be imagined. Upon her return to her home in Janesville, she gave one short glimpse of herself to the children at her mother's pre-kindergarten school. I recall her as being very thin and extremely reserved, probably out of a desire to avoid startling young children. She lived in the home with her mother where the school was located, and the happy sound of children at play could only have helped to restore her faith in humanity.

Marcia Gates later joined other veterans, some of them survivors of POW camps, in giving talks about their experiences to groups around Janesville. At one event, sixteen veterans, including Marcia Gates and Dale Lawton, spoke to a crowd of more than eight hundred in the auditorium at Janesville High School.[27] A few evenings later, the community again filled the auditorium to overflowing to witness the posthumous awarding of the Congressional Medal of Honor to Janesville resident Sergeant Gerald Endl, who had grown up in nearby Fort Atkinson. His young widow, Janesville's Anna Marie (Goethe) Endl, accepted on his behalf. Earlier, when details of the Bataan Death March atrocity had first been released to the press, the *Janesville Gazette* editorialized "Avenge Bataan!"[28] Feelings ran high in Rock County.

Janesville was the site of a German prisoner of war camp in 1944 and 1945. Camp Janesville, as it was called, was one of thirty-eight POW camps scattered throughout Wisconsin. Most German prisoners were moved to the United States and Canada, instead of being held in Great Britain, to deprive them of the means or hope of escape. German POWs held in America and Canada were fortunate. The United States and Canada had not suffered from Nazi bombs or invasions, as England and Russia had. So the United States and Canada were more inclined to provide good treatment for POWs than were the English or, more particularly, the Russians.[29]

Camp Janesville, located on the southwest side of town at the corner of Crosby and Western (now Rockport) Avenues, opened in June 1944 and closed in October 1945. The camp population ranged between 250 and 600 prisoners, out of a peak of around 20,000 throughout Wisconsin. They arrived from Fort Sheridan, Illinois, by train. Camp Janesville included a cookhouse, dinner tent, shower building, two-man tents, and a soccer field. The U.S. Army captain in charge lived in a mobile home. The compound was surrounded by a barbed-wire fence and snow fence and secured by guards in towers. The POWs were trucked under armed army guard to pick corn and work in canneries in nearby Stoughton, Whitewater, Fort Atkinson, Lake Geneva, and Evansville. The German POWs sometimes sabotaged the pea viners by overloading them. The private companies for whom the POWs worked paid the U.S. Army for their labor.[30] Additionally, the POWs were paid regular hourly wages. They were permitted to freely speak and assemble within the prison compound.[31]

Most Janesville area citizens quietly resented that German prisoners of war were living a comfortable and safe life nearby while thousands of local and area men were in combat zones. My mother shared those sentiments. Local teenagers would sometimes verbally taunt the prisoners. On a few isolated occasions, however, local teenage girls would become infatuated with the wrong uniform. Following World War II, the POWs held in the United States were repatriated to Germany. Some, however, were held under military jurisdiction until late 1946 to be individually screened for war crimes. One young American army private, Michael Kennedy of Chicago, recounted that he was assigned after the war to escort duty aboard a U.S. Navy transport ship loaded with German wartime POWs. The ship sailed from the United States, with prisoners and guards alike assuming that the men were being taken home to Germany. Then, as the ship entered the English Channel, it made a sharp left turn and docked in Southampton, England. Voicing much discontent, the prisoners were turned over to British military authorities to be individually screened for war crimes. Those who received clearance were returned home to Germany.[32] The blizzards and intense cold of the winter of 1944–45 were harsh in Wisconsin and throughout the Midwest. Railroad traffic was sometimes delayed. Troop movements were inhibited. Delivery of coal supplies for both war production and home heating were often slowed as well. Most homes in the 1940s were heated with coal furnaces. During the 1944–45 winter coal shortage, some people resorted to the 1930s depression-era trick of scavenging for pieces of coal that had been dropped by steam engines along railroad tracks. The frigid temperatures and blizzards of a Wisconsin winter were minor inconveniences, however, compared to the conditions that my father, along with hundreds of thousands of American soldiers, endured on the continent of Europe.

In December, my dad wrote to my mom in what seemed (to the censors) to be a response to one of her letters that she was "very fortunate" to have been able to take a guided tour of a B-29 bomber when it was on public display at the Madison airport, because "they are still pretty secretive about that plane." He then pointedly asked if she had been able to see a C-47, one of the planes that towed the gliders that Dad would ride to their combat landing zones.[33] Decades later, Mom did not recall having ever gotten aboard a B-29, and she would most certainly have remembered having done so. My dad had successfully slipped past the censors the information that the C-47 was important in his life. Thereafter, Mom knew to watch for news reports of combat operations involving the C-47.

About a week later, on December 19, 1944, Dad wrote, "I sure hope it's over before Christmas. It sure would be cause for a joyous holiday season."[34] Five days later, on Christmas Eve, Mom began to prepare the next day's turkey dinner for her parents and played a violin solo for the midnight service at St. Peter's Lutheran Church in Janesville. The same night, unknown to her, Dad was ordered into combat with the 17th Airborne Division. The Battle of the Bulge had broken out a few days earlier in the Ardennes Forest in eastern Belgium and Luxembourg. My father would fight in the largest and most costly single battle in American military history. As broadcaster Edward R. Murrow reported from London, the British people during the war would wish one another "So long" or "Good luck," but never a "Merry Christmas."[35]

SEVEN

"I'm Still OK— Somewhere in Belgium"

The Battle of the Bulge

*O*n Christmas Eve 1944, my father flew from England with the 17th Airborne Division to "Somewhere in France" aboard C-47 cargo planes. The division was then shipped at night from Charleville, France, by two-and-a-half-ton army trucks to the cold and snow of southern Belgium. Dad and his comrades were attached to General George Patton's Third Army during a drive from the south, toward Houffalize, Belgium, to flatten the Bulge and defeat the German counteroffensive. When they went into combat, they were flanked on the left by the 101st Airborne Division and on the right by the 87th Infantry Division.[1]

The Battle of the Bulge took place over a two-month period between December 1944 and February 1945. For some time, combat operations had been favorable for the Americans and their British and Russian allies. The Stalingrad victory in January 1943 and the D-Day invasion in June 1944 were the turn of the tide in Europe. Since then, British-American armies in the west and Russian armies in the east had steadily advanced on broad fronts toward the German homeland. By the end of 1944, Russian forces had pushed the Germans out of the Soviet Union and into eastern Europe. General Dwight Eisenhower's American-British-Canadian Allied armies had liberated France, Belgium, and most of Holland and were poised on the borders of Germany.

With the coming of winter, General Eisenhower in the west and Soviet Field Marshal Georgi Zhukov in the east slowed their advances in order to build up troops and supplies on the continent for a spring-time drive into Germany for the final victory. In the Ardennes Forest of eastern Belgium, American lines were thinned out. It was thought that if the Nazis were to launch an unlikely winter counteroffensive, they would surely not be so foolish as to come through the thickly wooded and snowbound hills of the Ardennes, where the roads were narrow and twisting.

On December 16, German forces launched a massive counter-attack through the Ardennes in eastern Belgium. Spearheaded by tanks, they planned to overrun American supply dumps to refuel and then drive the Allies into the English Channel. Speed and timing were vital to the huge German tanks, which would be halted if they did not reach their fuel resupply in time. In the first days, German armies executed their plan to perfection and inflicted massive allied casualties. They had punched nearly a seventy-five-mile "bulge" into Allied lines.

American and British field commanders were rapidly shaken from their pessimistic view of the situation by Generals Eisenhower and Patton. Whereas most commanders saw disaster, Ike and Patton saw opportunity. They recognized that the Germans had put their last remaining crack troops out into the open in a showdown battle. It was, by any measure, the largest battle fought by American armies in any war—larger than D-Day, larger than Midway, and larger than Gettysburg. But when the 101st Airborne Division held onto the Ardennes road hub of Bastogne, it slowed the German tank offensive. General Patton remarked at the time that "[t]he German has stuck his hand in a meat grinder, and I've got hold of the handle!"[2]

Three days after the Bulge broke out on December 16, the tone of my dad's letters reflected an urgent concern. He closed a short note to Mom by asking her to "[p]lease write often and understand if you don't hear too often from me. I'll write as often as I can." The men of the 17th Airborne Division at Camp Chiseldon believed, accurately, that they were about to be plunged into combat. On December 18, General Dwight Eisenhower ordered the 17th Airborne Division and the 11th Armored Division to move from England to the continent. The weather grounded the 17th Airborne Division's air transports and delayed their departure until December 24.[3] A few days later, Dad wrote, "I am still ok—somewhere in Belgium. Sherman was certainly right. Remember me in those prayers every night darling."[4]

The 17th Airborne, including my dad's 193rd Glider Infantry Regiment, began combat on the night of January 3 armed only with light weapons. Each soldier carried an M-1 rifle, two hundred rounds of ammunition at a time, and a few hand grenades. They went into combat against the battle-hardened and elite First SS Panzer (tank) Corps, which comprised the Twelfth and Ninth SS Panzer Divisions and two infantry divisions, including a brigade drawn from Hitler's household guards. The Twelfth SS Panzer Division had a deserved reputation for earlier brutality on the Russian front, as well as combat experience at Normandy in the weeks following the D-Day invasion in June 1944. Their commander would later be convicted of war crimes for his involvement in the Malmedy Massacre of American prisoners of war and Belgian civilians during the Battle of the Bulge.[5] My dad's 17th Airborne Division may have been one of the hands on General Patton's meat grinder, but the meat was tough grizzle.

It was frightening to American soldiers to see the dinosaurlike fifty-four-ton Tiger tanks, with their 88-millimeter guns, and the fifty-ton Panther tanks rumbling toward them through the falling snow and fog of the Ardennes Forest.[6] When American troops took refuge in woodlots, German tanks and artillery opened up with "tree-toppers" to create a hailstorm of flying wood splinters that killed and maimed as effectively as any shrapnel. The soldiers' desperate need to prevent their feet and hands from freezing was compounded by their efforts to keep their rifles from freezing up. German forces in the Bulge had experience fighting in the snow and cold of Russia. Initial American casualties were high. The winter weather, stinging wind, and drifting knee-deep snow were torture. Wounded men would die in the cold unless they were cared for within a half hour.[7] My dad made a classic understatement to my mom when he wrote, "You probably see pictures in the paper of all the snow and cold we are in."[8]

The 193rd Glider Infantry fought along a straight and narrow Ardennes road that ran northeast from Bastogne through the villages of Monty, Flamierge, and Flamizoulle to Houffalize, Belgium. The steadily inclining road became known as "Dead Man's Ridge." It ran parallel to the Ourthe River, which flowed through a deep valley and across the Ardennes plateau, where it entered the Meuse River near Liege. In the mile and a half between Monty and Flamierge, American troops attacked under cover of a wind-blown blizzard and, on the second day, faced a German counterattack led by tanks. In less than two days of fighting, some units of the 17th Airborne had suffered a frightening 40 percent casualty rate. Dad later described the conditions in a letter, saying that he had been "on top of a hill out in the open with snow to my knees and storm—half rain—half snow."[9]

On January 7, all three regiments of the 17th Airborne Division spearheaded the advance of General George Patton's Third Army toward Flamierge, located about five miles northwest of Bastogne. My dad's 193rd Glider Infantry, commanded by Colonel Maurice Stubbs, was on the right flank abutting the 101st Airborne Division. The 513th Glider Infantry was in the center and the 194th Glider Infantry on the left flank. To move more quickly through the knee-deep snow, the soldiers left their overshoes, packs, and coats behind. After the 17th took the village, the Germans retaliated with a barrage of anti-aircraft 88s, tanks, and artillery. Once the fighting subsided, 17th Airborne troops found themselves without their winter overwear and short on food and ammunition. The 193rd was hit particularly hard. General William Miley, the 17th Airborne commander, later remarked, "The situation had not changed. The enemy was still out there. . . . The weather was as forbidding as ever. There was almost no visibility and no chance of air support. You could still not observe artillery fire."[10]

The 17th Airborne's immediate food problem was partially alleviated when the men discovered an abandoned German army supply truck that contained enough to feed a nice chicken dinner to most of the division! The difference between German army and U.S. Army combat food was striking. American C rations and K rations provided a balanced and nourishing, if not especially tasty, diet. Although they were loaded with vitamins, they were canned, were usually eaten cold, and were seldom filling. Bill Mauldin, the *Stars and Stripes* cartoonist who created "Willie and Joe" wrote that "the German army was pretty well fed. Maybe they didn't know much about vitamins, but their stuff was filling. It was always a great day when our patrols found caches of [German] food."[11] So, the capture of a veritable culinary oasis with enough chicken to feed most of the 17th Airborne Division was very welcome.

The Germans continued their unrelenting counterattacks along Dead Man's Ridge with tanks, flamethrowers, and artillery "tree-toppers." It took the 17th Airborne four days of hard fighting, accompanied by unmerciful casualties, to advance a mile and a half to Flamierge, a small Belgian community that had been reduced to rubble.[12] German forces stubbornly held a line five miles west of Houffalize at the confluence of the two branches of the Ourthe River.[13] So the fighting continued.

In the Battle of the Bulge, the second enemy of American soldiers was the weather. Men needed to keep their feet dry in order to keep them warm. My dad remembered from training days at Camp Blanding that oversize shoes that were well-padded by heavy wool socks were preferable to tight-fitting footwear that cut off circulation. Whatever paper the soldiers could find they stuffed under their shirts and inside their shoes to serve as insulation. G.I.s from northern states who had shoveled snow or done outdoor work in the winter knew enough to keep their arms and legs moving, to rub their hands together, to wiggle their toes and noses, and to trap their breath under blankets or tarpaulins to maintain body heat and avoid frostbite. My dad was fortunate to have the heavy wool sweater that my mom and grandparents had mailed to him in England. Intended to be a bit of luxury in the damp chill of England, the sweater became a potential lifesaver during the freezing blizzards in the Ardennes Forest.

British Prime Minister Winston Churchill told the House of Commons during the Ardennes fighting that "we must not forget that it is to American homes that the telegrams of personal loss and anxiety have been going during the past month." My mother received one of those Western Union telegrams of "anxiety" from Adjutant General J. A. Ulio informing her that my father was "slightly injured in action nine January in Belgium. Mail address follows direct from hospital with details."[14] Pud Harper delivered the telegram to Mom while she was working at the Janesville pre-kindergarten school. Mom later recollected that "when I learned that your father had been wounded my initial reaction was that at least he would be coming home alive. I lived on hope."

My dad thought the injury was so minor that the War Department would certainly not send a telegram about it, so to avoid worrying Mom he did not inform her by letter. Indeed, the day after he was "slightly injured in action," he wrote "am o.k." from the field hospital, asked Mom if she was eating well, and said that his mail was arriving slowly. Two days later, he asked Mom if the bracelet he mailed her for Christmas had arrived safely. Not knowing the extent of Dad's injury was, of course, the most worrisome for my mother. She was as relieved as it is possible to be when Dad later told her the details of his injury in a letter.[15]

My dad had frozen his feet in the Bulge on January 9, an injury that afflicted more than 15,000 combat soldiers fighting in the damp cold, icy winds, and constant blizzards of eastern Belgium. For more than a month, men fought in the snow. They slept in the snow, which covered ground that was frozen too hard to dig adequate foxholes. They became weary from the constant exposure to the elements. And they died in the snow. My dad's injuries were, unfortunately, not serious enough to earn him a trip to England or the United States and away from the fighting.

Dad returned to combat after recovering for six days in a 17th Airborne forward aid station near St. Etienne, Belgium, and in a field hospital near Neufchateau, Belgium, run by the 224th Airborne Medical Company. When he returned to combat, the German forces opposite the 17th Airborne Division were no longer elite troops. On January 16, my dad's 193rd Glider Infantry Regiment, which had liberated the town of Houffalize and its stately old medieval castle, faced rag-tag but heavily armed German units made up of many last-ditch draftees and walking wounded, referred to as Volkssturm infantry units. Their officers lacked combat experience.[16]

From a comment Dad made in one of his letters, Mom surmised that he had been taken prisoner of war sometime during the week of January 20 but, after a few hours, had managed to escape from the ineffective German Volkssturm troops. With uncharacteristic sharpness, he pointedly wrote that "I would like to get a good German watch for myself. That's the only souvenir I want." Mom took the letter to Rock County Red Cross Director Mary Kamps, whose immediate interpretation of the remark was that he had indeed been taken prisoner, had his wristwatch stolen by his German captors, then escaped. In a subsequent letter, he again referred obliquely to having been taken prisoner. In response to a question Mom had written to him concerning the well-publicized German massacre of American prisoners of war near the Belgian village of Malmedy, Dad wrote that "[p]ractically the same thing happened to us that you wrote, but it is nothing to talk about. It's a messy business—that's all I care to say."[17]

When he returned to his comrades in Company B of the 193rd Glider Infantry, they were in combat in Luxembourg along the Our River near Eschweiler, north of Vianden, where they fought from January 27 until February 10. The Our River twists and meanders southward to eventually flow into the Moselle River. Dad and the troops of the 193rd Glider Infantry were among those given the mission to hold Skyline Drive, the main road between Luxembourg City and Aachen, Germany. Under the circumstances, they were unable to appreciate the majestic vistas of the wooded hills, rolling meadows, and picture-postcard villages in the scenic Our River region. They were being shot at, many of their buddies had been killed earlier in the Bulge, and they had lived in inhuman combat conditions since leaving Camp Chiseldon more than a month earlier. German forces on the opposite side of the Our River to the east were protected by nine-foot-thick concrete walls, pillboxes, bunkers, and barbed-wire tiers on the sloping east bank of the river.[18]

One day, my dad's Company B was able to take refuge in what he described as a "large warehouse with all the windows out." The temporary shelter was a welcome respite from the elements. Although Dad wrote that his company was able to spend some time in the warehouse, he did not add that the plentiful population of neighborhood rats also sought warmth in Company B's building and hundreds of others like it. As the fighting wore on, the mountains of snow from the month-long Ardennes blizzard melted during a February thaw, making the Our River an impassable torrent of rushing water.[19]

My father's letters, even during the Bulge, were focused more on home than on his own experiences. On January 10, the day after he landed in the hospital, he asked Mom, "Is Butch putting on any weight? And what about you? Are you preparing good meals for yourselfs." On January 18 he wrote, "Still in Belgium. . . . Heard that Fitzgerald's son was killed on Leyte. I've seen and been through a lot but want to forget it all as soon as I can." On January 20, he asked again whether the bracelet he'd sent her had arrived.[20]

The men of the 17th Airborne Division were unaware of it at the time, but they were caught in a high command controversy between their commander, General William Miley, and General George Patton. Patton recorded in his diary during the Battle of the Bulge that "[a] few days ago I was on the point of relieving . . . Miley. . . ." Patton faulted Miley for the heavy losses suffered by the 17th Airborne Division and unfairly accused Miley of not advancing fast enough while being faced with the best the German military had to offer.[21] Front-line combat soldiers, however, were disinterested in the identity of their top commanders. They were what Ernie Pyle described as "tired and dirty soldiers who are alive and don't want to die. . . ."[22] Their main concern was to survive the two simultaneous battles in which they were engaged, fighting German armies and brutal winter weather.

When German forces counterattacked through the lightly defended Allied lines of the Ardennes Forest, they had hoped to cross the Meuse River and drive to Antwerp and the English Channel. Snowstorms initially neutralized the American air advantage by preventing planes from taking to the skies to attack German tanks. The 101st Airborne Division's defense of Bastogne slowed the German advance, thus denying adequate quantities of gasoline to the fuel-guzzling Tiger and Panther tanks. The Bulge lasted for several weeks and became the costliest battle in American military history. The number of casualties and the intensity of the suffering was brutal.

In the long run, however, the Battle of the Bulge shortened the war and saved lives. The German army had used its best remaining tank and infantry units in the winter Ardennes offensive, and once defeated, they were no longer available to resist the coming invasion of Germany by American, British, Soviet, and other Allied armies. Total defeat of Germany became inevitable. The fatally wounded beasts of the country's Nazi regime, however, refused to surrender. More soldiers would die before the war finally ended in May 1945 when General Dwight Eisenhower's armies met allied Russian armies on the banks of the Elbe River in central Germany. More widows, from Stourbridge in England to Penza in Russia to Janesville in Wisconsin, would need to find the words to explain to their children that Daddy would never be coming home.

By February my dad was able to write that he "just took a shower—man it was wonderful." It was the "[f]irst I've had since we left England," forty-five days earlier. He also increased his army pay allotment to Mom with the understated explanation that "the need for money is not as great when we are up on the front."[23]

My dad was among the fortunate soldiers who had survived the Battle of the Bulge, the largest single military engagement in American history. Between 7,000 and 8,000 American troops were killed, more than 20,000 captured or missing, and between 33,000 and 48,000 estimated to have been wounded.[24]

Following the Bulge, my dad and the rest of the 17th Airborne Division were shipped on February 12 by "40 and 8" trains to a regrouping area near Chalons-sur-Marne, France. The "40 and 8" railroad boxcars, of World War I vintage, were designed to carry forty men and eight horses during a bygone time when army cavalry had still been on horseback. By the time the 17th Airborne Division rode the "40 and 8s" to Chalons, the cars carried more than forty men, but no horses for travel companions. En route, the train passed through Verdun and the Argonne Forest, sites of heavy World War I fighting. In a letter, Dad remarked of the scene that "you can still see some of the old trenches that have never been filled in." He wrote to Mom's parents that "Charles Holmen and Larry Owens need sales. 6 or 7 more in longs easy sold," the first letter of each word spelling out "Chalons, 6 or 7 miles."[25]

During the 17th Airborne Division regrouping in France, the remnants of Dad's 193rd Glider Infantry Regiment, which had been decimated in the Bulge, were folded into the 194th Glider Infantry Regiment. My dad was placed in Company K. The regimental commander was Colonel James Pierce, who in civilian life had been a Sunday school teacher in Troy, Pennsylvania.[26] The division began to prepare for the airborne fighting for which it had trained during the months at Camp Chiseldon. Construction battalions labored feverishly to build enough long runways in the vicinity to enable the large tow planes to take off with their gliders.

As a result of combat in the Bulge, my dad earned his Combat Infantryman Expert Rifleman's Badge, the highest of four rifle rating grades for combat soldiers, complete with the wreath denoting that the wearer had been in combat. Shortly after receiving it, Dad wrote to Mom, "Got my Combat Expert Infantryman's Badge this week. It's the nicest looking medal the Army has, I think."[27] He even drew a sketch

Dad, on right, with his friend Sergeant Henry Dorff at the 17th Airborne Division's regrouping and marshaling base near Chalons-sur-Marne, France. The photo was taken in early March 1945, after they had survived the Battle of the Bulge and just days before the air drop over the Rhine River at Wesel, Germany, where my dad would be killed. Dad and Dorff are wearing their paratrooper boots and baggy paratrooper pants. After enduring two months of combat, my dad's strained expression is especially noticeable when contrasted with earlier pictures. His insignia include the 17th Airborne Division eagle's talon shoulder patch and his Silver Wings and Combat Expert Rifleman's Badge with garland on his left chest.

of it in his letter. The award was created in November 1943 for soldiers "whose conduct in combat is exemplary or whose combat action occurs in a major operation."[28] Glider training missions helped integrate new replacements with the combat veterans from the Bulge. Airborne units, whether glider or parachute, differ from infantry in that they arrive on a battlefield from the air, land behind enemy lines, and in order to survive need to make a rapid linkup with advancing ground forces.

For my father and the other men of the 17th Airborne Division, the sunny but chilly springtime in France was a welcome respite from the six weeks of winter combat, frozen feet, and sleeping in snowstorms during the Battle of the Bulge. Daily activities that had once been so ordinary in civilian life became unimaginable luxuries that the men were able to appreciate and enjoy during their brief relief from combat. For the first time in a month and a half, they ate cooked food instead of cold canned field rations. Instead of foxholes, they lived in tents heated on chilly nights with the firewood they chopped with axes. Reporter Ernie Pyle wrote, "The American soldier is a born housewife. . . . I've seen the little home touches created by our soldiers in their barns and castles and barracks and tents all over."[29]

One evening, Dad told Mom that he was writing his letter to her "by candlelight in my tent, so I hope you (and the censor) can read it." Once their Christmas packages from home belatedly reached them, Dad and a few of his buddies pooled their resources one evening to create a treat for themselves: fudge made from canned milk, sugar, a chocolate D-bar, some nuts, and a gallon can to cook it on the stove in their tent. My dad, who enjoyed working in the kitchen at home, created the fudge recipe and coordinated the cooking. The kitchens and supply tents had electric lines strung through them, and Dad remarked that it "sure seemed swell to hear some music again" on the radio. One man even had a camera and film, so they took a few snapshots to mail home to their families. Entertainers Mickey Rooney and Marlene Dietrich put on a live U.S.O. show for the 17th Airborne Division during its encampment at Chalons.[30]

Some of the men were lucky enough to get forty-eight-hour passes to visit Paris. Although my dad never got to Paris, he did go on a detail through Reims to St. Quentin and back to Chalons, a bumpy but pleasurable 150-mile round trip by jeep. The jeep was described as being "as faithful as a dog, as strong as a mule, and as agile as a goat."[31] The trip to St. Quentin was an opportunity to get away from the encampment at Chalons for a day. En route, he appreciated the peaceful scene in the French countryside of "a lot of oxen being used by farmers in the fields." The ride through small farm villages was a reminder of a more tranquil life back home in Janesville. On the road, his army jeep passed several civilians riding bicycles, but nonmilitary cars were rare. He said "it was good to find someone from home" after he had met a Madison man named Betlach who had entered the army after working at the Lorraine Hotel a block from the state capitol.[32]

My dad wrote that he and his buddies were "sweating out the crossing of the Rhine" River until the American First Army breached the Rhine at Remagen, Germany, on March 7, 1945. Upon hearing the news of the Remagen crossing, a false sense of security descended upon the men of the 17th Airborne Division at Chalons. Dad wrote that he was "sure glad to hear about the Rhine crossing. I was afraid that the airborne was going to be needed for that."[33] His anticipation even extended to the "hope that we won't be stuck with South Pacific after this is over and that we won't have to stay over here too long."[34] Mom anticipated that if Germany surrendered within a few weeks, Dad could be home by July, and our family would be together again.[35]

EIGHT

"Airborne Mission Soon"

Crossing the Rhine

O n March 19, 1945, my dad wrote to my mom in their pre-arranged code, "Airborne Mission Soon." The first letters of his words conveyed the message, which the censors never caught. It said, "Am in really beautiful ozone training now easy. Meal in several seconds—I'm off now. Seldom overlook our noonmeals." He continued by telling that they had "some pretty good wieners and the strongest mustard that you ever tasted. Has horseradish in it and I believe of English origin." It was his last letter home.[1]

Within hours, the 17th Airborne encampment near Chalons, France, was closed down and sealed off. No mail would be allowed out until after the airborne crossing of the Rhine River at Wesel was launched on March 24. Security patrols around the perimeter of the base were increased. Officers, then enlisted men, were briefed and shown aerial photos of the landing zones for the upcoming mission. Rumors circulated around camp that Nazi SS troopers waited in force near Wesel for the arrival of the 17th Airborne, and that German civilians would also be armed and dangerous.[2] The evening before the battle, the men of the 17th were fed steak dinners with apple pie for dessert. They were given the opportunity to attend religious services. My father took Catholic communion. Many of the men, lost in their own thoughts, slept fitfully at best. Others exchanged nervous conversation or played cards. Most of them cleaned and checked their rifles out of habit. Before dawn, the men were awakened, ate breakfast, and began loading the gliders for takeoff on a windy and sunny Saturday morning.[3]

The Rhine River was the last physical barrier to British and American armies in their eastward drive to meet Russian armies somewhere in Germany and bring an end to the European war. General Dwight Eisenhower, the Supreme Allied Commander, called the Rhine "a formidable military obstacle."[4] In military scope, the less-well-known March 24, 1945, crossing of the Rhine River was nearly as large as the D-Day landings on France's Normandy Peninsula. Historian Russell Weigley described British Field Marshall Bernard Montgomery's preparations for the Rhine crossing as "the majestic deliberation of a pachyderm."[5] The number of men and the volume of ammunition and supplies rivaled D-Day. Eighty thousand troops were to be put over the Rhine on the first day.[6]

The 17th Airborne Division assault at Wesel was conducted in coordination with the British 6th Airborne Division, which took off from bases in East Anglia, England, as the 17th left from France. The Anglo-American landing zones were defended by three German divisions, including two infantry units and one parachute unit, plus artillery and anti-aircraft gunners.[7] The 17th Airborne mission was to land two miles north of Wesel on the high wooded ground to the east of Diersfordt, then link up with the British 15th Infantry Division and the British 6th Airborne Division to capture the bridges over the Issel River. My dad's 194th Glider Infantry Regiment was to land in the southern part of the 17th Airborne's zone and seize the nearby woods. During the two weeks before the crossing, British and American forces began laying a huge smokescreen along a more than sixty-mile stretch of the Rhine River bend in the Wesel region.[8]

Wesel was the hub of a railroad, highway, and canal network. The night before the Wesel assault, two hundred British Lancaster bombers reduced the city of 25,000 inhabitants to rubble in one hour with 1,100 tons of bombs. In addition, 1,200 U.S. Eighth Air Force bombers destroyed German jet bases within range of Wesel. Medium bombers and fighters attacked all other Luftwaffe bases in the region. Allied amphibious troops followed the bombardment by crossing the river with the support of 3,500 field artillery guns and 2,000 anti-tank and rocket launchers.[9]

Each of the 17th ABN's Waco gliders carried a pilot and thirteen men, who called the airborne contraptions their "flying coffins." The motorless gliders were constructed mostly of canvas, which covered a frame of thin welded-steel support tubes, a wood floor, and plank seats. They had large wingspans. Bombers and cargo planes towed the gliders, either singly or in pairs. According to my dad's sergeant and friend Henry Dorff, their glider was double-towed. The takeoffs were rough, especially in those gliders that were being double-towed (one tow plane for two gliders). To complicate matters, a few towropes snapped on takeoff, and occasionally a pair of the double-towed gliders collided with each other. French farmers in their fields and townspeople from nearby Chalons-sur-Marne were awestruck by the sight and sound spectacle of the huge American air armada lifting off from runways near their homes.[10]

The gliders were like flying cages with men trapped inside. Once the gliders were in the air, a constant and loud wind rushed from the wake of the tow planes, buffeting them like butterflies in a cyclone. Air pockets triggered sudden altitude drops, making it necessary for the troops to be strapped to their seats. Some soldiers became nauseous from air sickness, nerves, or both. Even without the enemy anti-aircraft and machine gun fire that began near the landing zone, the entire three-hour journey from Chalons to Wesel was an unpleasant ride, despite being as smooth as could be expected in a glider. The 17th Airborne's divisional history included the remark, "The sky had been full of praying men ever since this glider and hundreds like it soared off toward its bloody destination east of the Rhine."[11]

The air armada was a sight to behold. A three-and-a-half-hour steady stream of planes, coordinated from twenty-three bases in France and England, converged over Brussels before heading the one hundred miles to the landing zones around Wesel. The first wave was composed of C-46 and C-47 transports carrying paratroopers. Next came 1,348 American Waco and British Horsa gliders, two-thirds of which were double-towed. The tow planes included American B-17 and B-24 bombers, C-47 cargo planes, and British Lancaster, Halifax, and Sterling bombers. Nine hundred fighter planes flew air cover. By midday, the American 17th and British 6th Airborne Divisions had placed 21,680 men on the ground at Wesel by parachute and glider.[12]

The Wesel air drop was no surprise to German troops, who had been ordered to sleep in their clothes next to their anti-aircraft guns on the night of March 23. Even the *Janesville Gazette* carried a front page banner headline the day before the Wesel operation announcing "Allies Poised for Rhine Jumpoff."[13] On the eve of the Wesel landings, Berlin radio propaganda broadcast in English, "Hi, all you good-looking guys in the 17th Airborne Division there in France. . . . We know you're coming tomorrow and we know where you're coming—at Wesel."[14] German anti-aircraft gunners were members of the Luftwaffe, the German air force.[15] They had leveled their artillery to fire on Montgomery's ground troops as they crossed the Rhine earlier in the morning, and they kept the guns there when the gliders arrived on the ground.[16]

With the Rhine below, glider pilots cut loose from the tow planes for the descent to the landing zone. Gliders cut loose at only four hundred to eight hundred feet from the ground, dangerously low for tow planes to fly. At that altitude, anti-aircraft, artillery, and machine gun fire permeated the smoke-filled sky. Glider pilots approached the ground at steep angles because of the intensity of the fire directed at them. More than half of the canvas-shelled gliders were hit by German anti-aircraft flak or small arms fire. The 194th Glider Infantry was in the last of three waves to arrive at Wesel late that morning. My father and the other troops saw the recently plowed farm fields below them littered with wrecked gliders, dead soldiers, abandoned parachutes, burning buildings, and panicked livestock. Screams of men and farm animals were accompanied by roaring airplane engines and the explosions of artillery shells.[17]

During the air drop at Wesel, the canvas glider in which my dad was riding was hit by anti-aircraft fire and crashed. The wood floor shattered as the appropriately named Waco bounced and fishtailed out of control and to a halt. Men scrambled out the glider's exits the instant their flying cage became motionless on the ground, to avoid the hail of German rifle fire. A few weeks later, a full-page *Life Magazine* photo showed my father lying next to the glider wreckage, wounded in the head, neck, and chest, with a medical corpsman kneeling over him. His armored vest was on the ground beside him. He was wearing the non-regulation sweater that my mom and grandparents had mailed to him to keep him warm in England and that had protected him from the blizzards of Belgium during the Battle of the Bulge.[18]

Mom saw this full-page photo in the *Life Magazine* of April 9, 1945, three days after she received the telegram informing her of Dad's death. The photo shows my dad lying on the ground bleeding to death after being hit with shrapnel. The medic tending him has propped his head on a piece of glider wing, and the smashed glider is in the background. Grandpa Wolferman enlarged the photo on Forest Products Laboratory equipment to reveal the same leg scar that my dad always had and to confirm that the sweater was the one Mom and Grandpa and Grandma had mailed to Dad while he was in England. A medical journal that Mom saw in the home of her friends Dr. Sam and Alice Freitag carried the same photo, but without Dad's face obscured as it was in the *Life Magazine* edition.

My dad was one of 159 members of the 17th Airborne Division to be killed in action crossing the Rhine at Wesel on the first day alone. Eighty-one additional men were missing, most of them dead, and 552 more were wounded. By the end of the second day, March 25, the 17th Airborne Division had 393 killed and 834 wounded. Additionally, forty-one men of the IX Troop Carrier Command, which delivered the 17th Airborne to Wesel, were killed.[19] British 6th Airborne Division losses were even higher.[20] By comparison, the 30th and 79th American Infantry Divisions, which made the amphibious crossing on the same day, suffered only thirty-one casualties.[21]

My dad's squad leader, First Sergeant Henry A. Dorff, later wrote to my mom and described the events as best he could:

> I was your husband's squad leader in France and at the time of the airborne invasion of Wesel, Germany, we were in the same glider with twelve other men. After we crossed the Rhine we received a shell hit in the floor of our glider. After we were hit, I looked quickly to the rear and saw that quite a few of the boys were hit in the legs. Clyde was hit in the neck and fainted or was "knocked out" right away. He wasn't bleeding badly and came to right after we landed. When we did land, everyone made a scramble for the doors as the bullets were coming in through the sides of the glider and we had to get out fast! I can't give you any more information except that the medic was fixing him up as I left.[22]

Mom would not learn of Dad's death until the telegram came thirteen days later, on April 6, 1945. Several of her letters that never reached him were returned, having gained added poignancy. The day after he was killed, on March 25, she wrote a "Dear Sweetheart" V-mail letter:

> Today is Palm Sunday and I played my [violin] solo in church. It went off swell. The folks came down this morning and sat in church with Richard. He gave me a big smile as I marched out the aisle with the rest of the choir. I have heard the reports on the radio with commentators that were right with the Gliders, and gave a complete description of their landing on the east side of the Rhine. Even told how some of the gliders crashed. You could even hear the motors of the planes. . . .

I sort of wonder if this war in Germany might be over by the 23rd of April—what a wedding anniversary that would be for us darling.[23]

On April 4, 1945, two days before receiving the telegram reporting Dad's death, Mom wrote to him, "I was lucky enough to get a nice chuck roast. We had that for supper tonight with all the trimmings. . . . then we had apple cake for dessert." She continued by prophetically remarking that "in crossing the Rhine I believe you must have landed near Wesel." She concluded her one-page V-mail letter with the hope that "[m]aybe you can be home for Richard's 5th birthday" on November 1.[24]

By the time the 17th Airborne crossed the Rhine at Wesel with Field Marshal Bernard Montgomery's 21st Army Group, the airborne portion of the operation was militarily unnecessary. In the advance planning stages, it was logical that the main Rhine crossing be made in the flat northern part of the river in Montgomery's sector. During the months of Montgomery's slow pace of overly deliberate preparations from October 1944 until March 1945, however, the entire situation had changed. When Montgomery actually launched the attack, the mission assigned to the airborne forces could have been achieved by ground troops with much less loss of life.

At the time of the March 24 Wesel crossings, the American First Army had already penetrated far to the east of the Rhine from its Remagen bridgehead more than two weeks earlier. Three full army corps were east of the Rhine and had even captured a portion of the autobahn leading to Frankfurt. By mid-March, the Army Corps of Engineers had built more than sixty pontoon bridges across the Rhine in the ever-expanding Remagen bridgehead between Cologne and Bingen. Those bridges may not have been visually attractive, but they were functional in speeding the end of the war and saving lives. Additionally, General George Patton's Third Army had suffered only twenty-eight casualties when it crossed the Rhine at Oppenheim on March 22. In the ensuing four days, Patton raced one hundred miles eastward against minimal German resistance. Soviet Field Marshal Georgi Zhukov's forces were thirty miles from Berlin and about to launch a ferocious 22,000-gun pre-assault artillery barrage on the city.[25] Historian Stephen E. Ambrose wrote that "[f]rom the crossing of the Rhine to the end of the war, every man who died, died needlessly."[26]

American General Omar Bradley had a quiet disdain for British Field Marshall Bernard Montgomery. In his memoirs, Bradley wrote:

> Had Monty crashed the river on the run as Patton had done, he might have averted the momentous effort required in that heavily publicized crossing. Fourteen days of preparation had given the enemy sufficient time to dig in with artillery on the far shore. And had it not been for our bridgehead at Remagen, toward which the enemy had diverted a major share of his strength, the German might have massed sufficient resistance to make necessary Monty's use of the air drop.[27]

Bradley believed that earlier crossings had rendered unnecessary the air drop over the Rhine by the 17th Airborne and others. Even General George Patton, who held the 17th Airborne Division's General Miley in low regard, recognized that Miley was faced with a situation beyond his control, commenting that "[o]ne of the chief defects of an airborne division is the fact that it never has anything it needs after it lands—no tanks, no adequate artillery, no transportation."[28] The more diplomatic and less critical General Dwight Eisenhower said that "[t]he March 24 operation sealed the fate of Germany. . . . The northern operation was made in the teeth of the greatest resistance the enemy could provide anywhere along the river."[29]

Like most American soldiers, my father was not concerned with World War II's grand strategy. They were interested primarily in "an early end to all of this," in my dad's words, so they could return to their homes and families. Nonetheless, they were caught in the stream's torrents. Dad had expressed his hope that "the Russians continue to roll," because it would mean an earlier end to the war. Internal tensions within the high command during the Battle of the Bulge had affected the 17th Airborne Division. The air drop over the Rhine was, as General Omar Bradley and others said, not necessary.[30] Certainly, Field Marshal Bernard Montgomery made wrong decisions with tragic consequences in the operation in which my father was killed. Nevertheless, it was Hitler and the Nazis who started the war and then refused to sur-

Clyde Haney Is Killed in Action East of Rhine

Former Manager of Fox Theatres in Janesville

Pfc. J. Clyde Haney, 33, manager of the Janesville theatres for Fox Wisconsin corporation before leaving for service 14 months ago, was killed in action in Germany March 27, after his division had crossed the Rhine, according to a war department telegram received Friday afternoon by his wife, Mrs. Vera W. Haney, 714 McKinley street. Slightly injured in action in Belgium Jan. 9, where he was serving with the 17th airborne division of the army, Pfc. Haney returned to the fighting Jan. 11, and since then letters have reached Mrs. Haney regularly, telling when he entered Germany and when he crossed the Rhine.

The war department telegram read as follows:

"The secretary of war desires me to express his deep regret that your husband, Pfc. Haney, Joseph C., was killed in action in Germany 27 March 1945. Confirming letter follows. (signed) J. A. Ulio, the adjutant general."

PFC. J. CLYDE HANEY

2 Elkhorn Men Reported Dead

The day after the arrival of the "regret to inform" telegram on April 6, 1945, I picked up the *Janesville Gazette* at our front door, as I often did. When I saw Dad's picture on the front page, I excitedly ran to tell Mom that "Daddy's picture is in the newspaper." I recall that she gave me a big hug and thanked me for telling her. But I can only imagine what raw emotions she must have kept to herself at that moment for my sake.

render when the handwriting was on the wall after D-Day in June 1944, or for that matter, even earlier, following the Battle of Stalingrad in January 1943. The ultimate and total responsibility rests with them.

Weeks before he died, my dad wrote a "Dear Son" letter in which he said that he sure wanted to be home "with you and mommy, but we have to make the Germans quit fighting first—then maybe Daddy can come home. We will have some great times together when I do come home."[31] On April 6, my mother's friends Marcia Mills and Mary Kamps arrived with the telegram informing her that my father "was killed in action in Germany."

A Wound You Can Never Heal

*M*y mother recollected decades after my father's death, "It is a wound that I could never heal. All I could do is try to overcome it." After receiving the telegram on April 6, she replaced the Blue Star in the front window, indicating a household with someone in service, with a Gold Star to signify a combat death. By that time, the front windows of very many Janesville and Rock County homes contained gold stars. On the large portrait of my dad that hung on her living room wall, Mom placed a caption that read "Your Life is a Beautiful Memory; Your Absence a Silent Grief." She later commented, "My friends were so good and kind to me after your father was killed—Dorothy and Joe Zigler, Marina Bliss, Hazel Sorenson, Ellie Ehrlinger, Sam and Alice Freitag, Marcia Mills, Mary Kamps, and Doc and Lydia Hyde."

Six days after Mom received the "regret to inform" telegram, President Franklin Delano Roosevelt died at Warm Springs, Georgia. She recalled that, in a strange way, his death gave her some comfort in the knowledge that wartime sacrifices did not discriminate between ordinary soldiers and the Commander in Chief. My mother found herself a twenty-six-year-old widow with a four-year-old son to raise. She stiffened her resolve and returned to teaching at the pre-kindergarten school, giving violin lessons, directing the church choir, and keeping my father's memory alive for me.

Months after Dad was killed, the army returned his personal effects. In addition to his glasses, a compass, and a German army belt buckle, they included photographs of Mom and me, with his bloody fingerprints on them. As he lay on the battlefield bleeding to death, he was holding those photos in his hand. His last thoughts were of us. When he died, the anonymous medical corpsman who attended him was kind and considerate enough to return the photos to Dad's wallet.

When Germany surrendered in May 1945, public elation was muted because of the realization that the war was not yet over. Janesville businesses, including banks, restaurants, pharmacies, professional offices, and taverns, closed on V-E (Victory in Europe) Day. War workers remained on their jobs at General Motors, Parker Pen, and other vital industrial plants. Local churches held well attended "victory thanksgiving services" in the evening hours. There was an absence of celebration, however. The *Janesville Gazette* reported, "Flags, which flew in only a few spots during the heavy rain of the first hours of surrender day Monday, burst forth later in the day when weather cleared."[1]

Like the rest of the United States, Janesville celebrated the end of World War II when Japan surrendered in August 1945. Especially in Janesville, which had paid such a heavy price in the Pacific war with the tank battalion, a Congressional Medal of Honor recipient, and others, there could be no relaxing until a final victory. Much of Janesville greeted the news that two atomic bombs had been dropped on Japan with hope that the war would soon end. My mother later recalled "waiting and waiting for Japan's response and wondering if it would ever come. I had the radio on for every news broadcast and also in between."[2] With the turn of events in Japan, Americans could now dream that their men in uniform would come home to their families, and that no more of them would have to die in the anticipated invasion of Japan and its accompanying bloody Battle of Tokyo. People anxiously wondered about the fate of those still not accounted for among the Janesville 99. How many of Janesville's sons, husbands, and brothers would return home from captivity in Japanese prison camps? How many would not? How many local lives did the new and still-unfamiliar President Harry Truman save by his decision?

When Japan finally surrendered, on Tuesday, August 14, 1945, a spontaneous community party erupted in downtown Janesville along Milwaukee Street and Main Street. From around seven in the evening until midnight, downtown Janesville was a mass of cars blaring their horns, elbow-to-elbow pedestrians on the sidewalks, and ankle-deep debris of paper and confetti covering everything. Flags flew from car fenders. Residents rang every bell they could find, and some even made blasts of noise with air compressors. One man kept beating a bass drum throughout the evening. The crowd was described as happy and, everything considered, orderly. Police arrested a jail-full of people for their own protection, not because they were any threat to others. They were released the next morning.[3]

Church services were held throughout the city on victory evening and during the next day. War plants including General Motors and Parker Pen closed for more than two days. Taverns closed before sunset on the first evening.[4] Gasoline and vegetable rationing were ended throughout the United States.

A few minutes after the radio announcement was made of Japan's surrender, my mom's friend Marina Bliss drove up in her yellow convertible to take us to the celebration in downtown Janesville. Mom was reluctant to go, but we did get in the car for a ride around the downtown circuit. I remember the crowds, the noise, the car horns, and everyone smiling and waving. I also remember that my mom was so very quiet. As she later said, "I was hurt that I was unable to celebrate, but I was happy for those who could celebrate." A final heart-rending irony was that the formal Japanese surrender, to General Douglas MacArthur on September 2, 1945, aboard the USS *Missouri* in Tokyo Bay, occurred on what would have been my father's thirty-third birthday.

A week after the surrender of Japan, the banner headline in the *Janesville Gazette* told people to anticipate "Tires, Nylons, New Radios Soon!"[5] Parker Pen rapidly returned to making pens instead of shell casings. Janesville's General Motors plant correctly anticipated a backlog of consumer demand for new Chevrolets and converted to peacetime production by October. Meat rationing ended by late November in time for Thanksgiving, and four days before Christmas, the Janesville newspaper revealed that tire rationing would end on New Year's Day 1946.[6]

In December 1947, two and a half years after my father was killed, the army presented my mother with the decision of where he was to be permanently buried. Rather than open the wounds by returning his remains to the United States for burial in either Arlington National Cemetery or a private cemetery, she determined that the American Military Cemetery at Margraten, Holland, was the most appropriate place. About forty percent of Americans killed overseas during World War II are buried in fourteen military cemeteries in Holland, England, Belgium, France, Luxembourg, Italy, Tunisia, and the Philippines.

When my mother signed the papers to leave my father's remains in the permanent American Military Cemetery in Margraten, she promised herself that one day we would visit his grave together. I remember sitting with her as she signed the papers on her glass-topped walnut coffee table, which had been a wedding gift from her bridesmaids. She told me the contents of the papers she was signing, and she then told me that we would visit Margraten together someday. I was seven years old.

Although Mom and I had each made the trip to Holland earlier, our first visit together was in 1982, thirty-seven years after my dad's death. Mom's first visit had coincidentally been on what would have been dad's sixtieth birthday, September 2, 1972. By the time we visited the cemetery together on Memorial Day 1982, I had become a university history professor and Mom was again widowed. We flew from Chicago to Amsterdam and from there rode a train to Maastricht, only seven miles from the cemetery. After checking into one of the city's several immaculate hotels, we boarded a bus for the twenty-minute ride to the 65.5-acre cemetery on the outskirts of the farming village of Margraten in the rolling hills of Limburg province. At the cemetery, 8,301 American soldiers lie facing west toward home, and an additional 1,722 names are remembered on the Wall of the Missing. Forty pairs of brothers are buried at Margraten.[7] The tulip poplars and rhododendrons were in full springtime blossom when we arrived, and the surrounding farm fields had just been plowed and planted. Cattle grazed in neighboring pastures.

We arrived at the cemetery early, in advance of the large Memorial Day crowd. Cub Scouts and Brownies stood as honor guards next to the fifty state flags lining the reflecting pool in front of the *Mourning Woman* statue and the Wall of the Missing. After a visit to the chapel, we strolled to my father's grave, located in Plot D, Row 15, Grave 9. There we placed the flowers for which the Dutch vendor in Maastricht had firmly refused payment when he learned of their purpose. All 8,301 graves were decorated with American and Dutch flags for Memorial Day. As next of kin, we had reserved seats and watched the Memorial Day ceremonies under a Dutch-blue sky. Dutch Queen Beatrix's presence swelled the crowd to well over ten thousand, and the Netherlands Royal Army Band and U.S. Third Army Band played several selections. Queen Beatrix, the U.S. Ambassador, area burgo-

U.S. Army Photo, AFCENT Europe, for the American Battle Monuments Commission

Mom was unaware of the army photographer who caught her deep in thought during her first visit to Dad's grave at the U.S. Military Cemetery near Margraten, Holland. This moment was especially poignant because it would have been Dad's sixtieth birthday, September 2, 1972.

masters, Dutch wartime resistance veterans, and numerous others made brief remarks and laid seventy-five wreaths, followed by a U.S. Air Force missing man formation flyover and the playing of taps.

On any given day of the year, hundreds of visitors pay their respects at the American Military Cemetery. On a 1985 visit, Mom and I were invited by a bus full of Scottish tourists to ride with them as their "stowaways" from the cemetery back to Maastricht. On my first visit in 1973, U.S. Ambassador J. William Middendorf and his family joined me for a hike to the top of the chapel tower for a panoramic view of the countryside. Another time, Mom and I had chatted with a friendly couple for some time before they revealed themselves to be Senator and

The first time Mom and I visited Dad's grave in Holland together was on Memorial Day 1982. We fulfilled the promise that she made when she signed the papers to have him permanently buried at Margraten.

Mrs. Ed Zorinsky of Nebraska. General George C. Marshall, the wartime Army Chief of Staff, visited nearly all the American Military Cemeteries as Chairman of the American Battle Monuments Commission and remarked that "[e]ach site evoked old memories of . . . the young Americans who paid the highest price that war can exact. Yet the tribute I gave these men in my thoughts must remain an unwritten one, for words cannot capture or convey gratitude held so deeply."[8] We learned that on Memorial Day 1945 approximately thirty thousand Dutch citizens assembled at the cemetery. They arrived on that day by every imaginable conveyance, including bare-rimmed bicycles, farm horses, and buses.

Easily the most moving and authoritative conversation we ever had in Margraten was with a chunky Dutchman who wore a beret and smoked a cigar. He had been head caretaker for decades, and he helped organize the burials in Margraten in 1945 and again in 1949–50 when the permanent cemetery was created. He informed us that as the bodies arrived from the front lines in Germany, they initially were buried in linen sacks and the graves marked with wooden crosses. When the permanent cemetery was created, each body was exhumed and reburied in a bronze G.I. coffin. Slit trenches were dug, each soldier was individually buried, and one-at-a-time committal services were conducted by a Catholic priest, Protestant minister, or Jewish rabbi. White marble headstones were installed, and flags used in the services were mailed to each next of kin.

My mother and I are among the fortunate next of kin to have visited the cemetery that means so much to all those of us with loved ones buried there. It was reassuring to see for ourselves that Margraten is a beautiful place and lovingly maintained, and to know that the Dutch people have not forgotten.

After a visit to one of the American military cemeteries even before the war had ended, Ernie Pyle wrote a tribute that would reflect the thoughts of veterans and their families for decades to come:

> Medals and speeches and victories are nothing to them any more. They died and others lived and nobody knows why it is so. They died and thereby the rest of us can go on and on. . . . There is nothing we can do for the ones beneath the crosses, except perhaps to pause and murmur, "Thanks, pal."[9]

My father and the hundreds of thousands of American soldiers who died in World War II missed living through the unprecedented economic prosperity of the postwar decades. They never knew television, shopping malls, interstate highways, or cars with power steering. They never lived to see the America of Elvis-mania, the Super Bowl, or the popularity of pizza. As a baseball fan, my dad would have been among those who reveled in the Braves' fever that gripped Wisconsin when the team moved from Boston to Milwaukee. The Volkswagen Beetle craze and the longevity of Spam would have puzzled them. Astronauts landing on the moon and the eradication of polio would have filled them with pride. They would have smiled to see General

On our Memorial Day 1985 visit to Margraten, we met U.S. Senator and Mrs. Ed Zorinsky of Nebraska, who gave Mom a lapel pin of Dutch and U.S. flags and insisted on walking with us to Dad's grave to pay their respects. They were very kind and thoughtful.

Dwight Eisenhower, along with the many World War II veterans to whom Ike would pass the torch, elected to the presidency of the United States. The September 11, 2001, terrorist attacks upon the United States would have angered them to the extent that many might have tried to see if their old uniforms still fit. But most of all, they missed the pleasures of enjoying their families, watching their children grow to adulthood, and living out their normal life spans.

Mom and I moved to Madison in the spring of 1948 to be closer to her parents. She sold the prewar blue Oldsmobile that she bought in 1946 in order to make the down payment on a Vilas Avenue home and to buy a bicycle for me. On Vilas Avenue, I had a big back yard to play in, after Mom cleared many of the raspberry bushes and replaced them with grass. And I was lucky enough to have another big yard to play in at Grandpa and Grandma's home near Shorewood Hills. I attended Randall Elementary School on Regent Street, began piano lessons, joined the Cub Scouts, and spent time at Vilas Park Zoo. Because Mom had to be at her work desk at Madison General Hospital (now Meriter Hospital) on Park Street at an early hour, my morning chores were to wash the breakfast dishes, bring the milk in, talk to Grandma on the phone, hide the house key in the stairway landing, and walk to school. If I stayed overnight with Grandpa and Grandma, I would get a ride from Grandpa or ride the school bus. One summer, Mom and I borrowed Grandpa's car for a trip to Springfield, Illinois, to visit Abraham Lincoln's home. Following my high school graduation, Grandpa and I traveled in his black 1952 Chevrolet to the Black Hills, Washington, DC, and Toronto/Niagara Falls during three successive summers.

My grandparents, Chauncey and Mabel Wolferman, became very important people in my life. Mom and Grandpa and Grandma helped tremendously to fill the void in my life after my dad was killed. At a young age, they impressed upon me the importance of education and the opportunities available at the University of Wisconsin in whose shadow I was growing up. They often took me to the University of Wisconsin's Washburn Observatory for the public viewing sessions. We attended parades on the Capitol Square, one of which included President Harry Truman riding in the back seat of an open car and waving to the crowds. Thankfully, Mom and Grandpa and Grandma always talked about my dad to keep the memory of him alive in my mind.

This is one of only a few photos with Mom, Grandpa, Grandma, and me together, because one or the other of us usually took the family pictures. The occasion here is my college graduation day in 1963.

Mom remarried in 1951 to Percy Piddington, a widower with two sons close to my age. A large and muscular man, he had grown up on a southern Wisconsin farm. Percy's first wife had died suddenly of cardiac arrest three years earlier. He was the public school administrator at Ellsworth, Wisconsin, and then at Whitewater, Wisconsin. He eventually became the assistant registrar at the University of Wisconsin–Whitewater. In the first years of their marriage, curious community members would often ask of me and my stepbrothers, Scott and Bruce, which two were "his" and which one was "hers." The three of us delighted in confusing the issue by giving different answers each time anyone inquired. Percy Piddington, whom Mom often referred to as "my gentle giant," was a stable stepfather during my adolescence, and when I reached adulthood he became one of my closest and most reliable friends.

In the decades after the war, my mom's old Janesville friends went on with their lives. Joe and Dorothy Zigler lived in Janesville for many years, until Dorothy died. He then moved to Atlanta to be near his daughter, Nancy, and her husband, James Warner, the son of James Warner Sr., who had been the advertising manager of the *Janesville Gazette* during World War II. Marina Bliss and her husband eventually moved to Principia College in Illinois, where he was on the faculty. Mary Kamps remained in Janesville and continued to serve as the

Mom and my stepfather, Percy Piddington, a few months after their 1951 marriage and their move to Ellsworth, Wisconsin. Together they found happiness that neither thought they would ever have again after the hard losses they both suffered.

executive director of Rock County's American Red Cross chapter for several years. Central Café owner Jim Zanias died in Janesville in 1951, but he had been able to visit his native Greece after the war.

Marcia Mills continued to operate the Peter Pan Pre-Kindergarten School in Janesville. Her daughter Marcia Gates, who survived three years as a POW, suffered a return of her cancer a few years after the war and died much too young.[10] Ellie Ehrlinger was widowed with four young daughters to raise, and she continued her interest in music after she was remarried to Janesville M.D. George Gutmann. Everett "Pud" Harper, who delivered so many wartime telegrams, lived a happy retirement in Janesville. John Freitag, the young son of Dr. Sam and Alice Freitag, became an oceanographer with the University of Rhode Island. Carol Sorenson, the daughter of Hazel and Ted Sorenson, grew up with a deadly accurate putter in her hands to become an international womens' golf champion, winning the 1964 Curtis Cup and the 1964 British Womens' Amateur Championship. She was selected as Wisconsin Woman Athlete of the Year in 1964.

My maternal grandparents lived long and happy lives in Madison. Chauncey Wolferman completed thirty years as a paper chemist for the Forest Products Laboratory and retired in 1951. Mabel Wolferman continued to clerk at Baron's Department Store in Madison for a number of years. Following retirement, Grandpa took part-time work as a bookkeeper for a Madison bank, helped in the Madison City Treasurer's office at property tax collection time, and became a highway inspector for the Wisconsin State Highway Commission. Grandma tended her flower garden and Grandpa his vegetable garden, and they spent every holiday with us. He adopted the retirement hobby of chair caning for the benefit of family, friends, and shut-ins.

In addition to raising three boys, Mom remained active in community activities in both Ellsworth and Whitewater. She directed the church choirs at English Lutheran Church in Ellsworth during our five years there and then for twelve years at First English Lutheran Church in Whitewater. She regularly played violin solos at church into the 1990s, and she joined the nearby Milton Choral Union. During the summer months in Ellsworth, she drove the three of us and carloads of our friends to the closest community swimming pool in nearby River Falls several times a week. After four summers of being a taxi-mom, she invited several influential community leaders into her living room for the purpose of initiating plans for building what shortly thereafter became the Ellsworth Swimming Pool.

After her boys had graduated from high school, Mom became a member of the board of directors of the Fort Winnebago Surgeon's Quarters Museum located in Portage. She worked for a while in medical records at the Fort Atkinson Memorial Hospital and then at the University of Wisconsin–Whitewater Placement Services office. As my grandparents developed medical problems in later years, Mom and I regularly traveled to Madison to provide whatever help they might need and to enable them to continue to live in their own home.

Throughout her life, Mom treasured and regularly wore the bracelet that was my father's last Christmas present to her, inscribed with the words "All My Love Always, Clyde, England, 12-25-1944."

Mom's parents, my Grandpa Chauncey and Grandma Mabel Wolferman, in 1961 during their retirement years. To me, they were ageless and never looked or acted old. These were the years when Grandpa and I took summer trips in his 1952 Chevrolet, until later health problems kept them at home.

Despite her sadness over losing my dad, Mom devoted the rest of her life to spreading happiness and the beauty of music to everyone around her.

Mom was my best friend and confidant from the time my father was killed until her death fifty-eight years later. She always encouraged me in my personal and professional interests. After my stepfather died in 1981 at the relatively young age of sixty-nine following a two-year chain of health crises, Mom and I ate many of our evening meals together. We traveled together often, including several visits to the Netherlands to visit my dad's grave. Mom lived with me for the last four years of her life, when she developed medical problems that sapped her energy and limited her vision. I became her eyes and her hands.

The loss of my father in World War II certainly affected my life beyond the void created by his absence. My college education was partly paid for by Public Law 634, best described as a G.I. Bill for war orphans. The Maud E. Warwick Foundation of New York, a private agency that granted scholarships to war orphans for graduate school, made me a benefactor. As the only surviving son of a father killed in combat, I was fortunate to be exempt from the draft during the Vietnam War. Mom recognized before I did the necessity of urgently applying to my draft board for the "only surviving son" classification, and I am eternally grateful that she began the paperwork to achieve that end in time. Maybe coincidental to the loss of my father, and maybe not, I earned my PhD in twentieth-century American history from the University of

Mom and I were a close-knit pair from the day my dad was killed in 1945 until Mom's death in 2003. This photo was taken in her elegant and gracious home in 1998, when she was eighty years old. After she had been widowed for the second time, Mom always said how blessed she had been to have been married to two wonderful husbands. On her bedroom mirror Mom taped the notation "Do Everything with Love."

Wisconsin. I later graduated from the Post-Doctoral Military History Seminar of the U.S. Military Academy at West Point and from the National Security Seminar of the U.S. Army War College at Carlisle Barracks.

Most people living at the time remember where they were when they learned of Pearl Harbor, the Kennedy assassination, and the terrorist attacks on New York and Washington. I recall a sense of relief at twelve years of age when I learned one morning, while I was attending summer bible camp near Grantsburg, Wisconsin, that the Korean War armistice had been signed. I will never forget the intense emotions of sadness and anger that both my mother and I felt as we sat in front of television and watched the terrorist attacks against the United States unfold on September 11, 2001. And I remember vividly the day in 1945 when the telegram arrived to announce my father's death.

The American and Allied soldiers of World War II fought to bring an end to the war so they could return home to their families and communities. They wanted only to live happy and full lives. In letters home, my father was like most soldiers when he expressed those hopes and dreams. He wanted to put his feet under his own table. He wanted to play ball with his son. He wanted a regular hot bath and a piece of apple pie, a fresh tomato, or a malted milk.

According to historian Stephen E. Ambrose, the American soldiers of World War II were "the children of

Mom is wearing her treasured "All My Love Always, Clyde, England 12-25-1944" bracelet on her left wrist in this photo, taken on the day I received my PhD from the University of Wisconsin in 1970. I am so thankful that Grandpa and Grandma lived to see this day, too.

democracy and they did more to help spread democracy around the world than any other generation in history."[11] Their achievement in destroying tyranny and totalitarianism in the twentieth century parallels the preservation of the Union and the destruction of slavery in the nineteenth century. It is certainly true that "the children of democracy" achieved the abstractions of advancing democratic political principles and winning strategic military objectives. They can be proud of such lofty accomplishments. They reached those great horizons, however, in the process of striving toward the more limited goals of survival and homecoming.

World War II veterans who were fortunate enough to come home formed the core of what has often been called the "greatest generation." They were educated by the G.I. Bill. They became leaders in business, labor, entertainment, public service, and the clergy. They developed America's space program. They made lifesaving advances in medical science. The American people entrusted them with national leadership from the presidency on down for nearly half a century. They led America through the decades of the Cold War and helped sustain an unprecedented decades-long American economic prosperity. They helped Germany and Japan become responsible citizens of the world and willingly supported the Marshall Plan to reconstruct war-torn Europe. There is no reason to think that the World War II soldiers who were killed in combat could not have come home and added quality and quantity to the postwar achievements of their buddies.

From Rock County, Wisconsin, alone, at least 302 men were killed in World War II.[12] From Wisconsin, 8,390 men were killed, and a third of a million served in uniform. Add to those the nearly half million American World War II dead. My father, Clyde Haney, was one of them. Add the millions of soldiers who died in the service of England, Russia, Canada, and all other Allied nations. Add the six million Holocaust victims. Add the millions of civilians killed in the occupied countries. The number of lives it cost to rid the world of a tyrannical madman and his followers is staggering. Each one of those soldiers had a name and a story. Each one of them had a family and friends whose lives were changed. The impact of World War II upon mankind, one person at a time, cannot be measured.

Selected Letters

*T*he following letters represent a carefully chosen sampling of the nearly 220 letters my parents wrote during the last thirteen months of Dad's life. The letters reveal the devoted love that Mom and Dad had for each other and for me. They show Dad's unwilling transformation from a successful civilian businessman into a combat-tested citizen soldier. Most clearly, they reflect that the constant to which he always held was the importance of his family. Even letters he wrote from frozen foxholes focused more on home than on his personal situation.

Mom and I have reread Dad's letters a number of times over the years. Most recently, I read them aloud to Mom at the same time I read the first draft of *"When Is Daddy Coming Home?"* to her, just a month before her death in February 2003. Until the letters became part of this book, only Mom, my grandparents Chauncey and Mabel Wolferman, and I had read them. Out of respect and deference, not from any lack of interest, my stepfather, Percy Piddington, did not read them.

The letters are here transcribed exactly as they were written to retain their tone and substance. I have made no alterations in matters such as punctuation or spelling and have used ellipses to represent omissions of mundane matters that have no bearing on the substance of the story. For clarity, I have standardized the form in which the dates of the letters appear. Dad almost always signed his letters with a stylized "CH" for Clyde Haney, and I have kept that trademark intact in these transcribed versions.

I have donated to the Wisconsin Historical Society a complete photocopy set of these letters, although for now I retain possession of the originals. My parents' wartime letters are invaluable treasures to me, and I am not yet ready to relinquish them.

Clyde to Vera and Richard,
writing from Fort Sheridan, Illinois, 2-18-44

To My 2 "Honeys":

Well, Darlin, I'm in the Army now. We got here yesterday at 11:30 noon. Had lunch and "short arm inspec" then assigned to Barracks. Middle of afternoon we were issued all our clothes. We are only allowed to wear "Fatigue Outfit" now. Had picture taken of whole gang that came from Madison and Milwaukee. We are all in the same Barrack, we sure look like gang of convicts. Last night we had the movies on diseases. Was in bed about 10:30 and up at 5:30 this morning. Had breakfast—made our beds (I cut myself shaving) and went over for 2 hours of written examinations. After that the "Articles of War" were read to us and explained. Then we went to lunch. I went from there over to Post Exchange and got this paper and pencil for 65¢ and am now writing a letter and you know I'm standing up to write it so I hope you can read it. We have double decker bunks here (I grabbed a lower) and am writing this on the upper standing up. This afternoon we get classified and assigned to some outfit. Fix our insurance up and allotments etc. Then I guess we come back and get our clothes ready to ship home. (We all got big shoes and mine squeak.) . . .

. . . I don't know how long it will be before you get some money but don't do anything unless you write me first and I tell you to check on it. (FOR THE FIRST CHECK ONLY I MEAN.) I don't know whether I'll get week-end off or not yet. Also don't know how long I will be here. . . . They won't tell you anything.

Well, dear, I still haven't got an address so you can't write yet. I'll forward as soon as I get it. Going to quit for now. Will write tomorrow or Sat.

Say Hello to everyone for me.
HI RICHARD
(He'll recognize his name if you show it to him.)
Love Hugs Kisses
CH

Clyde to Vera and Richard,
writing from Camp Blanding, Florida, 2-22-44

Tuesday P.M.

Hello Darlings:

Well, Sweetheart, you sure got your wish for me going South. I am in Fort Blanding, Florida. It is only about a 100 miles from Georgia State Line, about 40 miles south of Jacksonville, Florida. I tried to tip you off when I called you that I was moving out of Sheridan but I don't know if you caught it or not. We were told that morning that we were being moved but did not know where to. We boarded the train at 7 P.M. Saturday and they routed us crazy as hell to get us here. We did not get here until 6 A.M. this morning. TUES. We spent about 60 hrs on the train and could not even get off to stretch. All of us are very tired. This is a very large camp taking in an area of about 35 miles and about 140,000 men stationed here. I will be here for 17 weeks for Basic Training.

We have not been assigned to a Battalion as yet so we have no address. They said that we would have an address within 2 days so I'll write it to you as soon as possible because I sure want to hear from you. This is strictly the bunk but there's nothing that can be done about it I guess. You should see all the men in here 35-36-37 years old with 4 and 5 children. I caught a cold on the train—hope I get over it soon. How's Richard's cold? I haven't had a chance to write to anyone yet but you and I mailed a card to Dad. They've kept us on the move and we did not dare mail anything from the train. That's a funny feeling—getting aboard a train and not knowing where you're going. . . .

I sure miss you and Butch. I sure hope that both of you keep in good health. Please write as soon as I send you my address. We don't have much free time. We are confined to Quarters for 3 weeks. We are miles from nowhere and there won't be much chance to ever go anywhere or do much except right here on the post. Shows every night here. Looks like we landed in a tough camp. Sergeants are tough as nails. . . .

Well, kiss Butch a dozen times for me and then have him kiss you a dozen times for me. Will write as soon as I get a permanent address tomorrow or Thursday.

Love Always,

CH

Clyde to Vera, writing from Camp Blanding, Florida, 2-28-44

Monday P.M.

Hi Sweetheart:

Well its getting tougher by the day. It's 9 P.M. and we just got through shaving and cleaning up. We were up at 6 this morning and went out to drill from 7:30 to 8:30 came in and changed uniforms in 10 minutes and went over to theatre where we were addressed by a General and a couple of Colonels. Then we went to class in "military dress and courtesy." Then we had lunch and over to another class for 4 hours covering military organization and venereal diseases. They showed some films on diseases. Then we got an hour of drill and then dinner. Then we had a class for an hour tonight on First Aid. Then we all had to clean our barracks. We finished up about 8:30.

I guess I forgot to tell you that we had chicken yesterday for dinner. We sure have got a good and considerate Mess Sergeant. We had lemon pie today.

All of us here in our barracks (15 of us in each barrack) were feeling a little low today. We all expected to get mail by today but only one fellow got a letter. AND IT WASN'T ME!!!

We go out tomorrow morning for some drill with a pack on our back—first time. It isn't so heavy though, about 25 pounds. It won't be so bad until we have to start carrying the rifle too. . . .

Well, darling, write to me and tell me all the news. How you getting along and how is Butch? I sure miss you both plenty. Home was never like this toots—that's for sure—be glad when I get back.

Good night Dear

Write soon.

CH

Clyde to Vera, writing from Camp Blanding, Florida, 3-7-44

Monday P.M.

Hello Darlin:

This will not be too long a letter tonight because I have about 6 minutes before "lights out." I just finished cleaning my rifle and I had a ton of sand in it. It took me 1 1/2 hours to clean it. I cracked my forhead on the damn thing today (don't laugh) it wasn't funny.[1] I cracked my head just along the eyebrow. They dressed it up in the dispensary. It wasn't so awful bad but it was so close to my eye. Luckily I didn't break my glasses. We were learning how to "Hit the dirt" and Belly crawl— Boy is it ever tough to cradle that rifle so not to get dirt in it and pull yourself forward on your elbows with the rest of you flat on the ground. Have to keep head down low too. I think I'm going to loose my belly with all this strenous exercise. . . .

I have to get up at 5 in the morning as I get my turn at K.P. They don't work it like they used to—everybody takes a turn at K.P. as the work has to be done and they alternate throughout the ranks. You hit it about once a month and 2 days in a row. So I didn't do anything wrong to win this great honor. . . .

How's Butch? Did you explain his letter to him from his Daddy? What did he say?—Oh-oh Sergeant just yelled lights out

Bye for now Dear.

Love

write

CH

Clyde to Vera, writing from Camp Blanding, Florida, 3-16-44

Thursday P.M.

Hello Darling:

Oh Man—am I sore and stiff and tired and dirty. Have to go clean up and shave after I finish writing you. How's my (our) Butch? I didn't get any mail today but I got letters from you—Dad—and Don yesterday. Toots this is the nuts. Yesterday morning we went out to a training area and had to start from a certain point by 4's and go through a wooded area and swamps using a compass and supposed to come out at a certain place 1 1/2 miles away. Then we started from a different spot over there and took a different asthmus and came back through the swamp and woods to another stake. I was about 100 yards off on one trip and 25 yds on the return. THEN LAST NITE we did the same damn thing in the dark. We never changed clothes from the morning and we were in water up to our thighs both in the morning and at night. Sopping wet. We finished and got back to company area at 11:15 last night. Up this morning and the first hour was spent in hand to hand fighting. Throwing each other around. Then we threw hand grenades for 2 hours. This afternoon we strained our muscles trying to get in the 5 different G.I. positions to fire the rifle. DO I ACHE. About 15 of us were just interviewed again tonight. Some Lt. from classification. All he asked was how old I was, if I was married and if I had any children, what I did in civilian life, how much schooling I had, what Platoon I was in and how did I like the Army. I don't know what it was for or all about.[2] The Army doesn't tell you anything. . . .

We are getting a new company commander. Our Captain was moved up to Battalion Headquarters. 2 of our Corporals and one sergeant were transferred to a camp in Arkansas. Looks like they move these guys around every-so-often.

Well, darlin, I have to go shave and clean up and get to bed. I'm plenty done in tonight. I got a Easter card for you tonight at the P.X. and am sending it now so it won't get lost or mussed up, I was afraid that they would run out of them if I waited until Easter. Hello Richard: If you are a good boy for Mama and tell her that you love her and Daddy—I will send you a picture of Daddy next week,

Bye dears
write soon.
Love,
CH

Clyde to Vera and Richard, writing from Camp Blanding, Florida, 3-22-44

Wednesday P.M.

Hello Darlings:

I'm going to start this now but I don't know if I'll have time to finish it tonight or not. We work tonight you know. They are going to work us Saturday afternoon too so there won't be any passes this week-end. It's been raining like the devil here for about a half hour. A Regular downpour. We just finished supper. Well I was appointed squad leader by our platoon sergeant today so if I make good and am able to take this training (which I doubt) in all phases in good shape I may have the opportunity of becoming a Corporal in a short time after the 17 weeks of basic training is over.

I've had it plenty tough so far. Two of the boys from my hut came down with the mumps—one about 2 weeks ago and the other one this morning. They both went to the hospital. When anyone is sick and misses 7 consecutive days training they are taken out of their company and put in another cycle. We have spent every morning this week on "Dry Range" which is learning the different positions for firing the Rifle and how to sight the target and how to squeeze the trigger. We go through all the motions but without ammunition. I guess the actual firing comes in the next two weeks. They say we spend 1 whole week on the Range trying for scores. They have 5 different positions we use and I am no good for 2 of them. I'm too stiff in my middle. They make us use muscles in these positions that we never have used before and they are plenty stiff and get awfully sore. The boy that wrote home for his camera got it today but the P.X. here has not had any film for a week. You might stop in People's Drugs and ask Emmett Doyle if he would remember me and sell you a couple rolls of Kodack #116 films. If he has it and nobody's looking he'll sell it to you. Be sure and see him and ask him quietly so that no one hears you, understand? You send them to me if you can get them and I'll take some pictures for you. Well you will be starting on the job tomorrow—good luck, darling, I hope you make good at it and like it.[3] Write me all about it. I've got about 2 minutes left before we fall out and I have to get my pack on so I better sign off for now so I can get this in the mail tonite. Bye Bye for now. Kiss Butch and love him for me.

Love Always
Hubby

Clyde to Vera and her parents, Chauncey and Mabel Wolferman, writing
from Camp Blanding, Florida, 6-21-44

Wednesday Noon

Dear Sweetheart & Folks:

Well this part of it is just about over. It has been really tough at times. Incidentally, you better not write me here anymore as I expect to be shipped first part of next week and I probably would not get your letter. It sure is going to be swell getting home even if it's only for a few days. It's about all I've been thinking about for the last few weeks. . . . I'll either telephone you—or if I don't have time between the time I find out & when I leave—I'll wire you when I'm leaving. Well, there just isn't any news, dear, and I'm going to rest a bit until we fall out so will say bye for now and will write again Sat or Sun.

All My Love

CH

Clyde to Vera, writing from Camp Blanding, Florida, 6-25-44

Sunday P.M.

Dear Sweetheart:

Well, darlin, all I can think of now is getting on the choo choo for home. I <u>believe</u> I will leave here early Wed morning and hope to arrive either Thursday night late or sometime Friday. I'm sure anxious to see you and Butch. . . . We have been awfully busy this week checking in equipment and we worked all week to boot. This, I found out, is the biggest Infantry training camp in the country but I'm glad to get out of it. . . . I know that I'll have 10 days at home so you start planning on how you and where you want to spend them, darling. . . .

. . . Tell Butch I'm coming home to see him and he is to say hello Daddy real loud when he sees me get off the train. I'll wire, darlin, as soon as I know when I can get there.

All My Love

CH

Clyde to Vera, written 7-22-44 [4]

Saturday P.M.

Dear Sweetheart:

I am fine and arrived at my new station today. All I can say is that I am Somewhere on the East Coast. We are not permited to say where. It will be impossible for me to telephone you Sunday, tomorrow as we planned. I hope you didn't stay up half the night waiting for the call. I expect to go overseas sometime in the not too far distant future.

I want you to keep the old chin up and not to cause yourself a lot of excessive and unnecessary worry. I know that you can do it because we have had tough situations together before and I'll feel a lot better if I know that you're taking it as it comes and waiting and hoping for my early return. . . . I made another investment with the fellows this afternoon while we were waiting for instructions and was very fortunate. I am going to try and get a money order or check for another $50.00 and send to you. I think I was more surprised than you will be in getting the money.

Butch is our everything, dear, take good care of him—be good to him (I don't have to tell you that) but still make him mind. I don't know just when or how often I will be able to write but will as often as possible. You have my address on this envelope so keep them coming fast and furious. Bye for Now

with All My Love.

CH

Clyde to Vera, V-mail written 8-2-44

Hi Sweetheart: Still Somewhere in the [censored]. My stomach was doing the Jumpin' Jive for a couple days but feel pretty good today. Hungry as the dickens. Have a craving for 2 things but they don't go together—Sauerkraut and Liver. There are a couple fellows on board from Green Bay and also one from Fon[d] du Lac. I haven't heard from Dad since I was home but was thinking about him yesterday. Has he completed the pool yet? That's an ideal place for a pool if Ballard's don't copy the idea. Tell him to write me and I'll do so when I can. Tell Mom that I got Uncle Mike's letter alright.[5] I hope you are writing a lot so that when the letters do finally catch up with me I'll have lots of them. I can't tell you anything about the trip so will close for now.

   Love always.
   CH

Clyde to Vera, written 9-9-44

Dear Sweetheart:
Well, Darlin, I haven't written for a few days as I've been pretty busy. Much to my surprise, and I imagine you too, I awoke one morning at 3 A.M. to find myself in the "Airborne Infantry" Glider troops. Yup thats me. I am now assigned to a regular outfit. I can't tell you anymore than that but I imagine that's quite enough. Don't worry though as it's not nearly as bad as it sounds. I certainly gained in one respect in the move as I am at least comfortable now. Much better living conditions. . . . I will be wearing a slightly different uniform from now on—similar to the Paratroops—BUT I DON'T JUMP.[6] How's Butch? Does he miss me much or ask many questions? . . . There isn't any news except what I started with—so will close for now with All My Love. Keep the ol' chin up and write.

   Kisses & Hugs for Butch.
   CH

Clyde to Vera, written 9-30-44

Hello Sweetheart:

Well here I am again. I haven't written all week as I haven't been feeling too good and we had a couple night problems. I feel pretty good now so will be more regular. I got two letters from you yesterday and 2 from Mom. I only wrote the V mail those few times because that was all the paper I had or could get. This paper that I have now is not so good—it takes inks very badly. I still have my pen & pencil OK but I was out of ink for a while. . . .

I'm going to get a few hours in London Sunday. Haven't seen any flys around here. Mike was stationed about 40 miles from Southhampton but moved to within about 35 miles of where Ted was, at Oxford. No I don't need any cigarettes. I imagine you are having quite a time getting your Marlboroughs now.[7]

Darling, I'll try to send you $25.00 in a few days but thats all I can manage right now. The greater portion of the money I referred to went its merry way while I was on the boat. I didn't have a chance to send it before I left the States. If you have to dig into the saving go ahead. Write soon.

All My Love
Clyde

Clyde to Richard, written 10-29-44

Hi Butch—How's my boy? I know that by the time that you and Mommy get this letter that your birthday will have passed—but I want you to know that Daddy was thinking of you even if he is a long ways away from you. I hope you had a nice birthday. You have Mommy sit right down and write me a letter telling me all about it—what presents you got—and all about your birthday cake with all the candles on it. Daddy will get you a nice present as soon as he gets home from the Army. How's the football coming? Can you tackle Mommy? Hug & kiss Mommy for me. Bye to My Boy.

Daddy

Clyde to Richard, written 12-7-44

Hi Butch!

Are you being a good boy for Mommy while Daddy is away? You'll have to help Mommy like Daddy does when he is home!!! When Mommy gets ready to get the tree—you get right in her way and help her decorate it. I bet I know what Santa brought you for Xmas—but you write to me and tell me all about it. I thought your picture was just swell. You must have held real still while the photographer took it. Give Mommy a great big hug and a kiss for me.

Love to My Boy
Daddy

Clyde to Vera and Richard, V-mail written 1-8-45

Darlings:

Just a few lines to let you know that I am still OK—Somewhere in Belgium. Sherman was certainly right. Remember me in those prayers every night, darling. How's Butch? Got 2 letters from you yesterday written Nov. 30. How are the Folks and Mom? Don't worry Sweetheart and take good care of yourself.[8]

All My Love
CH

Clyde to Vera, V-mail written 1-12-45

Dear Sweetheart,

Still OK but cold in Belgium. I imagine the wrath of winter has descended upon good old Wisc. by now. Darling, I can't write as often as I would like but will as often as I can to you and you in turn will have to keep Mom and the folks advised. Explain to them that I can't get around to everyone like I used to and of course you come first. I hope the situation changes soon. Love to Butch and all. Did you get Bracelet—Butch's Ring and my wings?[9]

All My Love
CH

Clyde to Vera, written 1-27-45

Dear Sweetheart:

I haven't had a chance to write you in almost a week now so will try and make up for it now. Looks like we are staying where we are for the day so I have some time. I am now in Luxembourgh. You probably see pictures in the papers of all the snow and cold we are in. I haven't had any mail in 8 days except 1 letter. . . . As far as news is concerned you are getting it before we do as our papers here on the front are 3 days late. I sure hope the Russians continue to Roll. I picked up a pair of cuff buttons in a warehouse where we are this A.M. and am sending them to Dad as a novelty. Have you received your bracelet—wings and Butch's ring yet? I lost my watch—tell you about it when I get home—so—I'm looking forward to finding a good one on some Jerry. I don't know of anything that you could have sent me for Xmas that would have taken the place of the pictures of Butch and you. You have no idea how many times I look at them. . . .[10]

The V mail that you have been getting will have to do while I'm up here, dear, I hope you can read it as writing conditions are very poor. I picked this paper up here this morning on the floor. Oh yes—I am now a PFC—one striper. Will close for now with All My Love.

Hugs & Kisses to you both.

CH

Clyde to Richard, written 2-9-45

Dear Son:

Daddy received your letter yesterday so will answer it now. I was sure glad to hear from you and you told me lots of things, didn't you? Mommy told me all about you helping her carry the Xmas tree home and helping her trim the tree with the ornaments. Did you have a good time up at Grandma & Grandpa's house. What about that kittie they tell me you have so much fun with? I sure would like to have been home with you and Mommy but we have to make the Germans quit fighting first—then maybe Daddy can come home. We will have some great times together when I do come home. Take good care of Mommy for me—give her a big kiss now. Daddy has to go now so good-bye for now.

Daddy

Clyde to Chauncey and Mabel Wolferman, V-mail written 2-12-45

Dear Mother & Dad:
Am back Somewhere in France at a rest camp. Of course we don't know
for how long. We came back in the old "40 and 8 Style" without the 8
of course. Living in tents now instead of Fox Holes—and I like it much
better. Dad, Charlie Holman and Larry Owens need sales. 6 or 7 more
in longs easy sold—so see what you can do—eh?[11] I don't need anything and of course boxes don't come up to us when we are on line they
hold them for us until we get back aways so don't send anything now.
Will write more in couple of days. Love
    CH

Vera to Clyde, written 2-28-45[12]

Wednesday night

Dear Sweetheart:
Received your letter dated Feb. 15 saying that all that was the matter
with you was frost-bitten feet. I am certainly much relieved. You have
no idea—the things I thought of. I thought possibly it might be a
schrapnel wound in your leg, arm, or back. Or maybe a bullett in your
shoulder. Or possibly some broken bones. I am certainly relieved, darling. Only next time you're hospitalized I think it would be better for
<u>you</u> to write me right away—& then I won't have to wonder—because
the suspense is no fun. I didn't say anything to you before, but ever
since I got that telegram I've had one bad headache after another. I controlled my outward emotions wonderfully but it welled up inside of me
and consequently I had headaches. Today—my headache has left me
completely & I feel relaxed for the first time. You see—I thought it
might be most anything—& <u>not knowing</u> was worse than if it had
been more serious. The not knowing & trying to imagine & figure out
what it might be was harder on me that if you had had a real bad
wound. So much for that. It's all over now & I'm glad. Too bad you
couldn't have been hospitalized for a longer time though—then you
would have been out of the fighting. That thought also was what paci-
fied me I guess.

Tonight—Richard said—"I'm sure going to surprise Daddy, I'll be so big when he comes back—he's taking so long at the Army." . . .

. . . <u>Everyone</u> asks about you. What division are you with? They are certainly rolling the Germans back in the <u>Cologne</u> <u>area</u>!? . . . Will sign off for now.

All our love,
Vera & Richard

Vera to Clyde, V-mail written 3-7-45

Dear Sweetheart:

Thought I would try out a V-mail letter. This is the first one I have ever written. Let me know how long it takes to get it, & how you like it. . . .

Richard is fine & dandy. He just got out of bed & crawled up in the cupboard & got himself a donut & took it back to bed with him. . . . The War news has been quite encouraging the last 2 days. Are you up in the front lines again? I suppose so. Well, darling, the end of this paper comes too soon. I'm going to write some more in an Air mail tonight too.

All Our Love,
Vera & Richard. XXOO

Vera to Clyde, V-mail written 3-9-45

Friday night

Dear Sweetheart:

Since nursery school has closed temporarily, I have been flooded with calls from mothers wanting me to take care of their children. I have taken one or two when I could. . . .

The war news sounds encouraging. Are you across the Rhine yet? What <u>division</u> are you in? Are you with the <u>first</u> Army? Maybe the Jerrys will be finished in a few weeks, then I can look for you home by July. Think it might be possible? There are many rumors flying around here, but I'm inclined to think there will be some fierce fighting by the Jerrys as a last stand. That may be quite a <u>long</u> & bloody battle. [Censored] Richard is full of the dickens. He says that when you come home you have to get him a baseball, bat & a baseball glove & then play baseball with him on the sidewalk. I asked him where Daddy was going to get all these things & he said "Gambles—I saw some there." I didn't even see them—but <u>he</u> did. Night night. All our love,

Vera & Richard

Clyde to Vera, written 3-19-45

Dear Sweetheart:

Just recv'd. your letter written Feb. 22 telling me about seeing the Hydes'. First mail I've gotten from you in 2 weeks. No, I have not received the cable yet. As far as the Pfc is concerned—It means Private First Class and I got it after the Bulge. It is the grade between buck private and Corporal. Doesn't mean much. I measure the same around the chest. Practically the same thing happened to us that you wrote but it is nothing to talk about. It's a messy business—thats all I care to say.[13] Also got letter (V mail) from Doc this noon and he said you are looking swell. Sure glad to hear it. There isn't much news so will add a note to Dad.

All My Love, darling:
CH

<u>Dad</u>: Am in really beautiful ozone training now easy. Meal in several seconds—I'm off now. Seldom overlook out noonmeals.[14]

Well I'm back again—had some pretty good weiners and the strongest mustard that you ever tasted. Has horseradish in it and I believe of English origin.—oh yes—back to Vera again—I sent a package yesterday, dear, the crusafix goes to your Mother as souvenier from Luxembourgh. Also the snail-shells as a token from the fields of France. The buckle is off the belt of a German (now dead) and if Dad would really like to have that—let him have it. It came from the Bulge. The other—keep yourself. I also sent a few coins and paper money in letters. Did you receive them yet. . . . Still have not made it to Paris. Well, dear, no other news for now. Take good care of Butch & yourself and don't worry.

    Again & always

    All My Love.

    CH

Vera to Clyde, written 3-21-45

Wednesday night

Dear Sweetheart:

. . . The radio news commentator, Kaltenborn, said on the radio tonight that there were several airborne divisions ready to go into action on the east side of the Rhine River. So I suppose that means you. Unless you are already there. Are you with the 17th Airbone Division of the 1st Army? <u>Please answer</u> this. I'm anxious to know. . . .

    All Our Love,

    Vera & Richard

Vera to Clyde, V-mail written 3-25-45

Sunday night

Dear Sweetheart:

Today is Palm Sunday & I played my solo in church. It went off swell. The folks came down about 9:30 this morning & sat in church with Richard. He gave me a big smile as I marched out the aisle with the rest of the choir. I have heard the reports on the radio with commentators that were right with the Gliders, & gave a complete description of them landing on the east side of the Rhine. Even told how some of the Gliders crashed. You could even hear the motors of the planes. The radio commentators say that the soldiers of the Glider Infantry are "the finest fighting men of the war." I haven't had any mail from you for nearly 2 weeks now, I think they must be holding it up for awhile while this big push across the Rhine is going on. I sort of wonder if this war in Germany won't be over by the 23rd of April! What an anniversary that would be for us, darling.

All Our Love,
Vera & Richard

Vera to Clyde, V-mail written 4-4-45

Wednesday night

Dear Sweetheart:

. . . If I'm correct—by the papers—you were with the outfit that help get the 101st Airborne division out of the trap they were in. Also—as far as I can estimate, you are in the 1st Airborne Army—17th division fighting next to the 30th division of the 9th Army. In crossing the Rhine—I believe you must have landed near Wesel. Am I right? Let me know. On the radio tonight Kaltenborn suggested that Pattons 3rd Army might meet the Russian front within 5 days, thus cutting Germany in half, if our supplies could keep up with the speed at which the 3rd Army was progressing.

Richard is sound asleep right now. He was happy to be back to nursery school. Well, darling, no more news here. I must get to bed now. Write as often as you can. Maybe you can be home for Richard's 5th birthday. All Our Love,

Vera & Richard

Notes

Chapter 1

1. Many of the recollections throughout this book are those of my mother, Vera (Wolferman) Haney Piddington. Additionally, I remember many things from my childhood. And I am thankful that Mom always talked about my father and her experiences during the war to keep the memories alive. Clyde Haney's birth record is in the Minnesota Division of Vital Statistics, Winona County for 1912, number 34374. His death is recorded in the Dane County Wisconsin Register of Deeds, volume 240, p. 25, of Miscellaneous Records, number 60882. Vera Wolferman's birth record is in Dane County, Wisconsin, Register of Deeds, September 12, 1918, p. 379. Her death record is in the Jefferson County, Wisconsin, Register of Deeds, February 5, 2003. My father is buried in the United States Military Cemetery at Margraten, Holland, Plot D, Row 15, Grave 9, where the American Battle Monuments Commission also has his death record.

Chapter 2

1. Stephen E. Ambrose, *Americans at War* (Jackson, Mississippi, University of Mississippi Press, 1997) p. 143; William Tuttle Jr., *Daddy's Gone to War: The Second World War in the Lives of America's Children* (New York, Oxford University Press, 1983), p. 154.

2. *Janesville (Wisconsin) Gazette,* December 6, 1941. The *Janesville Gazette* was a valuable source of information for material throughout this book.

3. *Janesville (Wisconsin) Gazette,* April 9, 1942.

4. *Janesville (Wisconsin) Gazette,* April 15, 1942.

5. Michael Du Pre, *A Century of Stories: A 100-Year Reflection of Janesville and Surrounding Communities* (Janesville, WI: *Janesville Gazette,* 2000) p. 91.

6. Ibid., p. 93.

7. Vera Haney Piddington recollections; *Janesville (Wisconsin) Gazette,* December 1, 1942 and March 22, 1944.

8. *Badger Quarterly* (University of Wisconsin student newspaper), September 1945; Du Pre, *A Century of Stories,* p. 93.

9. *Janesville (Wisconsin) Gazette,* August 9, 1945 and April 14, 1942; Du Pre, *A Century of Stories,* pp. 90 and 92.

10. *Janesville (Wisconsin) Gazette,* December 11, 1941; Du Pre, *A Century of Stories,* p. 90.

11. William Fletcher Thompson, *The History of Wisconsin, vol. 6, Continuity and Change, 1940–1965* (Madison, State Historical Society of Wisconsin, 1988), p. 94.

12. Industrial Commission of Wisconsin, Statistical Department, Statistical Release No. 268 entitled "Manufacturing Industries in Janesville [Wis.];" Du Pre, *A Century of Stories,* pp. 79 and 90.

13. Thompson, *The History of Wisconsin,* p. 96.

14. Du Pre, *A Century of Stories,* p. 94.

15. Ibid., pp. 97 and 99.

16. *Janesville (Wisconsin) Gazette,* November 24, 1940 and June 2, 1944; Du Pre, *A Century of Stories,* p. 84.

17. *Janesville (Wisconsin) Gazette,* November 25, 1940; Du Pre, *A Century of Stories,* pp. 93 and 95. Janesville's World War II community spirit experienced a rebirth following the terrorist attacks on the World Trade Center and Pentagon on Tuesday, September 11, 2001. On the following Saturday at the American Red Cross Blood Drive station on the Janesville Mall, there was an estimated three-hour wait for people to donate blood.

18. Du Pre, *A Century of Stories,* pp. 92–94.

19. *Janesville (Wisconsin) Gazette,* May 26, 1944.

Chapter 3

1. Vera Haney Piddington quoted in *Janesville (Wisconsin) Gazette,* December 25, 1994; Selective Service, "As the Tide of War Turns: The 3rd War Report of the Director of Selective Service, 1943–44" (Washington, D.C.: Government Printing Office); Selective Service and Victory: "The 4th Report of the Director of Selective Service" (Washington, D.C.: GPO, 1948).

2. Clyde Haney to Vera Haney, February 18, 1944.

3. Clyde Haney to Vera Haney, February 23, 1944; Clyde Haney to Mae Haney, July 15, 1944. Mae Haney was Clyde's biological mother. He was raised by his step-grandfather and his grandmother, Ike and Lydia Sharp.

4. *Infantry Replacement Training Center Handbook* (Special Service, Infantry Replacement Training Center, Camp Blanding, Florida, 1944), pp. 3–4, 14–15.

5. Ibid., p. 5.

6. Clyde Haney to Vera Haney, February 23 and 25, 1944; Clyde Haney to Mae Haney, March 7 and 27, 1944.

7. Clyde Haney to Mae Haney, March 7, 1944; Clyde Haney to Vera Haney, March 12, April 8, and May 6, 1944.

8. Clyde Haney to Vera Haney, March 1 and 6 and April 11, 1944.

9. Clyde Haney to Vera Haney, March 1, 6, 7, 12, and 23, 1944.

10. Ibid., March 1, 6, and 7, 1944.

11. Ibid., April 8 and 10, 1944; Clyde Haney to Mae Haney, March 7, 1944.

12. Clyde Haney to Vera Haney, March 12, 1944.

13. Ibid., April 3, 1944

14. Clyde Haney to Vera Haney, February 27, March 6, 12, 21, and April 8, 1944. I sure did look and ask for my dad—constantly.

15. Ibid., March 17, 1944.

16. Ibid., April 10 and May 15, 1944.

17. Vera Haney Piddington quoted in *Janesville (Wisconsin) Gazette,* December 25, 1994.

18. Stephen E. Ambrose's *Americans at War* is an excellent source on the impact of World War II upon American society in general.

19. Clyde Haney to Vera Haney, April 8, 1944.

20. Clyde Haney to Vera Haney, April 8, May 7 and 15, and June 21, 1944.

21. Ibid., March 1, 20, and 23, 1944.

22. Ibid., March 20 and May 3, 1944; Clyde Haney to Mae Haney, April 17, 1944.

23. Ibid., May 6 and 15, 1944.

24. Ibid., June 9, 1944.

25. James Pleyte Jr. to Richard Haney, October 28, 2003.

26. Clyde Haney to Mae Haney, March 7 and 27, 1944; Clyde Haney to Vera Haney, May 15, 1944; Clyde Haney to Carl Bunce, a Janesville friend, May 7, 1944.

Chapter 4

1. Clyde Haney to Vera Haney, June 26 and 30, 1944.

2. *Janesville (Wisconsin) Gazette,* June 6–7, 1944; Du Pre, *A Century of Stories,* p. 96.

3. Clyde Haney to Mae Haney, July 15 and 26, 1944.

4. Clyde Haney to Vera Haney, July 17, 21, 22, and 24, 1944. Pinpointing the timeline for my father's movements in the army is simply a matter of matching his letters home with D. R. Pay's *Thunder from Heaven: The Story of the 17th Airborne Division 1943–1945,* the official divisional history (Birmingham, Michigan: *Boots, The Airborne Quarterly,* 1947), p. 27.

5. Clyde Haney to Vera Haney, August 2, 1944.

6. Pay, *Thunder from Heaven.* News broadcaster Edward R. Murrow crossed the Atlantic on a troop ship in July 1943 and described the experience in a subsequent radio broadcast. See Edward Bliss Jr., editor, *In Search of Light: The Broadcasts of Edward R. Murrow 1938–1961* (New York: Avon Books, 1967), pp. 81–85.

7. Ernie Pyle, *Here Is Your War* (Chicago: Consolidated Book Publishers, 1944), pp. 4–6. Ernie Pyle, the G.I.s' favorite syndicated newspaper columnist who lived and wrote about ordinary soldiers, also crossed the Atlantic on a troop ship and recorded his observations in his classic book.

8. Clyde Haney to Vera Haney, March 1 and August 2, 1944; Clyde Haney to Mae Haney, July 27 and August 10, 1944.

9. Pay, *Thunder from Heaven;* Bliss, *In Search of Light,* pp. 81–85.

10. Pyle, *Here Is Your War,* p. 4.

11. Clyde Haney to Vera Haney, August 2, 7, and 15, 1944; Bliss, *In Search of Light,* pp. 81–85.

12. Ibid.

Chapter 5

1. Clyde Haney to Vera Haney and to Chauncey and Mabel Wolferman, August 7, 1944; Clyde Haney to Vera Haney, August 10 and 15, 1944; Clyde Haney to Mae Haney August 25, 1944.

2. Clyde Haney to Vera Haney, August 8 and 10, 1944; Clyde Haney to Rev. Charles Puls, the pastor who married Clyde and Vera at Luther Memorial Church in Madison, November 26, 1944.

3. Clyde Haney to Vera Haney, August 15 and November 22, 1944; Clyde Haney to Chauncey and Mabel Wolferman, October 23 and November 20, 1944.

4. Angus Calder, *The People's War: Britain 1939–1945* (New York: Pantheon Books, 1969), p. 371.

5. Clyde Haney to Vera Haney, October 3, 1944.

6. Clyde Haney to Vera Haney, August 10, September 1, 9, and 18, October 6, 15, and 29, and November 20, 1944; Clyde Haney to Chauncey and Mabel Wolferman, August 7, 1944; Clyde Haney to Mae Haney, August 27 and 30, 1944; Clyde Haney to Charles Puls, November 26, 1944.

7. British Information Services, *Britain against Germany, 1939–1945* (New York: British Information Services, 1945).

8. Clyde Haney to Vera Haney, August 21, October 6 and 15, and November 10, 1944; Clyde Haney to Chauncey and Mabel Wolferman, November 9 and December 7, 1944.

9. The Times of London, *Britain's Homage to 28,000 American Dead* (London: The Times, 1952), p. 6.

10. Clyde Haney to Vera Haney, August 15 and 27 and November 7, 1944; Clyde Haney to Chauncey and Mabel Wolferman, November 9, 1944; Clyde Haney to Mae Haney, December 17, 1944.

11. Clyde Haney to Chauncey and Mabel Wolferman, September 9 and November 9, 1944; Clyde Haney to Vera Haney, September 30 and October 23, 1944; Pay, *Thunder from Heaven,* p. 17.

12. Pay, *Thunder from Heaven,* p. 17; Clyde Haney to Vera Haney, September 9 and October 6, 1944; Clyde Haney to Chauncey and Mabel Wolferman, November 20, 1944.

13. Ernie Pyle, *Brave Men* (New York: Henry Holt and Company, 1944), p. 305.

14. Clyde Haney to Vera Haney, September 30 and October 3 and 30, 1944; Clyde Haney to Chauncey and Mabel Wolferman, December 7, 1944.

15. Clyde Haney to Vera Haney, September 18, 1944.

16. Clyde Haney to Vera Haney, September 30, October 3, 11, and 23, and November 15, 1944; Clyde Haney to Mae Haney, September 30 and October 23, 1944; British Information Services, *Britain against Germany.*

17. Calder, *The People's War,* pp. 223–225.

18. Marquis Childs, "London Wins the Battle," *The National Geographic Magazine* (Washington, D.C., National Geographic Society, August 1945); Edward R. Murrow, quoted in Bliss, *In Search of Light,* p. 104.

19. Calder, *The People's War,* p. 172.

20. Clyde Haney to Vera Haney, August 10, September 1 and 18, October 3, 6, 15, 23, and 29, and November 25, 1944; Clyde Haney to Chauncey and Mabel Wolferman, November 9, 1944; Clyde Haney to Mae Haney, August 27 and 30, 1944.

21. Clyde Haney to Vera Haney, November 3 and December 7, 1944; Clyde Haney to Richard Haney, December 7, 1944.

22. Edward R. Murrow, quoted in Bliss, *In Search of Light,* p. 106.

Chapter 6

1. Vera Haney to Clyde Haney, February 28, 1945. Of the letters my mother wrote to my father, the ones that survive are those that were returned to her because they did not reach him prior to his death.

2. Vera Haney to Clyde Haney, March 2, 1945.

3. Vera Haney to Clyde Haney, March 9, 1945.

4. Vera Haney to Clyde Haney, March 19, 1945.

5. Clyde Haney to Vera Haney, March 21, 1944; Clyde Haney to Mae Haney, March 27, 1944.

6. Vera Haney Piddington recollections.

7. *Janesville (Wisconsin) Gazette,* September 15, 1944, and August 21, 1945.

8. Clyde Haney to Vera Haney, December 7, 1944; Vera Haney to Clyde Haney, March 27, 1945; *Janesville (Wisconsin) Gazette,* February 6, 1945. Carol Sorenson later became an international golf champion, winning the British Open and the Curtis Cup, among other competitions.

9. Vera Haney to Clyde Haney, March 27, 1945.

10. Vera Haney Piddington recollections.

11. Vera Haney to Clyde Haney, March 7, 12, and 15, 1945.

12. *Janesville (Wisconsin) Gazette,* August 15, 1945.

13. Cpl. Edwin S. Mills Jr., "Will We Get Jobs after the War?" *Yank: The Army Weekly,* July 1943, p. 8.

14. *Janesville (Wisconsin) Gazette,* October 16, 1944; Du Pre, *A Century of Stories,* p. 96.

15. Vera Haney to Clyde Haney, March 7, 1945.

16. Clyde Haney to Vera Haney, December 7, 1944.

17. Vera Haney to Clyde Haney, April 2, 1945.

18. *Janesville (Wisconsin) Gazette,* March 19, 1945, and July 31, 1999.

19. Vera Haney to Clyde Haney, March 7, 1945; *Janesville (Wisconsin) Gazette,* March 20, 1945.

20. Dale R. Dopkins, *The Janesville 99: A Story of the Bataan Death March* (Janesville, WI, Minuteman Press, 1981), p. 40. Dopkins was one of the Janesville 99.

21. Vera Haney to Clyde Haney, February 28, 1945; *Janesville (Wisconsin) Gazette,* February 4, 1945; Olga Gruhzit-Hoyt, *They Also Served: American Women in World War II* (New York: Birch Lane Press, Published by Carol Publishing Group, 1995),

pp. 10–11; Marian Nicely, "The Nurses of World War II," *The American Legion Magazine,* September 1995, p. 22.

22. *Janesville (Wisconsin) Gazette,* February 6, 1945; Nicely, "The Nurses of World War II," p. 22.

23. Douglas MacArthur, *Reminiscences* (New York: Crest Books, 1965), pp. 284–285.

24. MacArthur, *Reminiscences,* p. 285; *Janesville (Wisconsin) Gazette,* February 6, 1945; Nicely, "The Nurses of World War II," p. 22.

25. MacArthur, *Reminiscences,* p. 286.

26. Virginia (Gates) Munns, Tucson, AZ, to Richard C. Haney, March 2, 1992. Virginia Munns was the twin sister of Marcia Gates; *Janesville (Wisconsin) Gazette,* February 6, 1945; Nicely, "The Nurses of World War II," p. 22.

27. *Janesville (Wisconsin) Gazette,* March 22, 1945.

28. *Janesville (Wisconsin) Gazette,* January 28, 1944.

29. *Janesville (Wisconsin) Gazette,* June 20, 1944; Betty Cowley, *Stalag Wisconsin: Inside World War II Prisoner of War Camps* (Oregon, WI; Badger Books, 2002), pp. 165–171.

30. *Janesville (Wisconsin) Gazette,* June 20, 1944; Cowley, ibid.

31. Richard B. Stolley, ed., *Life: World War II: History's Greatest Conflict in Pictures* (Boston: Little, Brown and Company, 2001), p. 224.

32. Cowley, *Stalag Wisconsin,* pp. 165–171; Michael Kennedy, interview with author, Whitewater, Wisconsin, 2001.

33. Clyde Haney to Vera Haney, December 12, 1944.

34. Clyde Haney to Vera Haney, December 19, 1944.

35. Edward R. Murrow quoted in Bliss, *In Search of Light,* p. 58.

Chapter 7

1. Clyde Haney to Vera Haney, February 15 and 25, 1945; Pay, *Thunder from Heaven,* p.19; Charles B. MacDonald, *A Time for Trumpets: The Untold Story of the Battle of the Bulge* (New York: Bantam Books, 1985), p. 617.

2. George S. Patton Jr., quoted in *Life Magazine,* June 5, 1995, p. 15.

3. MacDonald, *A Time for Trumpets,* p. 561; Hugh M. Cole, *The Ardennes: Battle of the Bulge* (Washington, D.C.: Department of the Army, Office of the Chief of Military History, 1965), p. 560.

4. Clyde Haney to Vera Haney, December 19, 1944, and January 8, 1945. His reference to Sherman was regarding Civil War General William Tecumseh Sherman's remark that "War is hell."

5. Charles B. MacDonald, *The Last Offensive* (Washington, DC: United States Army Center of Military History, 1993), pp. 34–35; MacDonald, *A Time for Trumpets,* pp. 610, 645, and 648–649; Cole, *The Ardennes,* p. 647.

6. Cole, *The Ardennes,* p. 652.

7. Ibid., p. 650.

8. Clyde Haney to Vera Haney, January 27, 1945.

9. Clyde Haney to Mae Haney, February 17, 1945; Pay, *Thunder from Heaven,* p. 21.

10. William Miley, quoted in Clay Blair, *Ridgeway's Paratroopers* (Garden City, NY: Dial Press, Doubleday and Company, 1985), p. 412; Bill L. Taylor, Lafayette, Indiana, to Richard C. Haney, April 20, 2003. Taylor was a soldier in the 17th Airborne Division, 193rd Glider Infantry Regiment.

11. Pay, *Thunder from Heaven,* p. 22; Blair, *Ridgeway's Paratroopers,* p. 413; Bill Mauldin, *Up Front* (New York: Henry Holt and Company, 1945), p. 172.

12. Pay, *Thunder from Heaven,* p. 22; Blair, *Ridgeway's Paratroopers,* p. 413.

13. MacDonald, *A Time for Trumpets,* p. 610.

14. Ulio the Adjutant General to Vera Haney, Western Union, February 1, 1945; Winston Churchill, quoted in William K. Goolrick and Ogden Tanner, *The Battle of the Bulge* (Chicago: Time-Life Books, 1979), p. 189.

15. Clyde Haney to Vera Haney, January 10 and 12 and February 15, 1945.

16. Pay, *Thunder from Heaven,* p. 28; MacDonald, *A Time for Trumpets,* pp. 654–655.

17. Clyde Haney to Vera Haney, February 19, 1945; Clyde Haney to Mae Haney, January 27, 1945; Clyde Haney to Vera Haney, March 19, 1945.

18. Ibid.; Pay, *Thunder from Heaven,* p. 26.

19. Clyde Haney to Vera Haney, February 19, 1945; Clyde Haney to Mae Haney, January 27, 1945; Pay, *Thunder from Heaven,* p. 26; Mauldin, *Up Front,* pp. 151–153.

20. Clyde Haney to Vera Haney, January 10, 18, and 20, 1945.

21. George Patton, quoted in Martin Blumenson, *The Patton Papers 1940–45* (Boston: Houghton-Mifflin, 1974), p. 627.

22. Pyle, *Here Is Your War,* p. 304.

23. Clyde Haney to Vera Haney, February 7 and 8, 1945.

24. R. Ernest and Trevor N. Dupuy, *The Encyclopedia of Military History* (Cambridge: Harper and Row, 1986), p. 1114; Dwight D. Eisenhower, *Crusade in Europe* (Garden City, New York: Doubleday and Company, 1961), p. 386.

25. Clyde Haney to Chauncey and Mabel Wolferman, February 12, 1945; Clyde Haney to Mae Haney, February 17, 1945.

26. William B. Breuer, *Geronimo! American Paratroopers in World War II* (New York: St. Martin's Press, 1989), p. 555.

27. Clyde Haney to Vera Haney, February 25, 1945.

28. Clyde Haney to Vera Haney, February 25 and March 5 and 14, 1945; Clyde Haney to Mae Haney, February 25, 1945; "Images and Decorations of the U.S. Armed Forces," *National Geographic Magazine* (Washington, DC: National Geographic Society, December 1, 1944).

29. Pyle, *Here Is Your War,* p. 133.

30. Clyde Haney to Vera Haney, February 19 and 25 and March 10, 11, and 14, 1945; Clyde Haney to Chauncey and Mabel Wolferman, March 11, 1945.

31. Pyle, *Here Is Your War,* p. 289.

32. Clyde Haney to Vera Haney, February 12, 19, and 25, 1945.

128 NOTES TO PAGES 78–84

33. Clyde Haney to Mae Haney, March 7, 1945; Clyde Haney to Vera Haney, March 10, 1945; Clyde Haney to Chauncey and Mabel Wolferman, March 11, 1945.
34. Clyde Haney to Mae Haney, March 15, 1945.
35. Vera Haney to Clyde Haney, March 9, 1945.

Chapter 8

1. Clyde Haney to Vera Haney, March 19, 1945. The rest of the message is less clear, but a reasonable interpretation is that the German troops facing the 17th Airborne Division will be pretty good, and the strongest mustard might imply the anticipation of hard fighting. Possibly the horseradish of English origin reference is to the fact that the 17th Airborne was attached to the 21st Army Group commanded by British Field Marshal Bernard Montgomery.
2. Breuer, *Geronimo!* pp. 541–542; John Toland, *The Last 100 Days* (New York: Bantam Books, 1967), p. 301.
3. Burton C. Betow, "D-Z Minus Ten," *The Lutheran Journal* (Edina, Minnesota: Outlook Publications, J. W. Leykim, 1:53, 1986), pp. 18–19; Toland, *The Last 100 Days,* p. 301.
4. Eisenhower, *Crusade in Europe,* p. 411.
5. Russell Weigley, quoted in Stephen E. Ambrose, *Citizen Soldiers* (New York: Simon and Schuster, 1997), p. 419; Pay, *Thunder from Heaven,* p. 43; Breuer, *Geronimo!* p. 558.
6. MacDonald, *The Last Offensive,* p. 297.
7. Toland, *The Last 100 Days,* p. 310.
8. Pay, *Thunder from Heaven,* pp. 35 and 39; Field Marshal The Viscount Bernard Law Montgomery of Alamein, *Montgomery of Alamein: Normandy to the Baltic* (New York: St. Martin's Press, 1948), p. 383.
9. Franklin Davis Jr., *Across the Rhine* (Chicago: Time-Life Books, 1980), pp. 83–84; Dupuy, *The Encyclopedia of Military History,* p. 1117; Blair, *Ridgeway's Paratroopers,* p. 452.
10. Pay, *Thunder from Heaven,* p. 43; Telephone conversation by Richard C. Haney with Henry Dorff, Minneapolis, Minnesota, May 16, 2003.
11. Pay, *Thunder from Heaven,* p. 43.
12. Davis, *Across the Rhine,* pp. 85, 96, and 113; Blair, *Ridgeway's Paratroopers,* p. 455; MacDonald, *The Last Offensive,* p. 309.
13. *Janesville (Wisconsin) Gazette,* March 23, 1945.
14. Breuer, *Geronimo!* pp. 542–543.
15. Ambrose, *Citizen Soldiers,* p. 419.
16. Vera Haney to Clyde Haney, March 25, 1945.
17. Blair, *Ridgeway's Paratroopers,* p. 459.
18. *Life Magazine,* April 9, 1945, p. 33.
19. Betow, "D-Z Minus Ten," pp. 18–19; Pay, *Thunder from Heaven,* p. 33; MacDonald, *The Last Offensive,* p. 313.

20. Toland, *The Last 100 Days,* p. 310.

21. Eisenhower, *Crusade in Europe,* p. 412.

22. Henry A. Dorff to Vera Haney, quoted in *Janesville (Wisconsin) Gazette,* March 20, 1946.

23. Vera Haney to Clyde Haney, March 25, 1945.

24. Vera Haney to Clyde Haney, April 4, 1945.

25. R. Ernest Dupuy and Trevor N. Dupuy, *The Encyclopedia of Military History,* p. 1120; *Life Magazine,* June 5, 1995, p. 18; *The American Legion Magazine,* September 1995, p. 40; MacDonald, *The Last Offensive,* p. 294; Stephen E. Ambrose, *Eisenhower and Berlin, 1945: The Decision to Halt at the Elbe* (New York: Norton and Co., 1967), p. 47.

26. Stephen E. Ambrose, *The Victors: Eisenhower and His Boys: The Men of World War II* (New York: Simon and Schuster, 1998), p. 330.

27. Omar Bradley, *A Soldier's Story* (New York: Henry Holt and Company, 1951), p. 524.

28. George S. Patton Jr., *War As I Knew It* (Boston and New York: Houghton-Mifflin, 1947 and 1975), pp. 211–212.

29. Eisenhower, *Crusade in Europe,* p. 414.

30. Clyde Haney to Vera Haney, January 27 and February 19, 1945; Clyde Haney to Chauncey and Mabel Wolferman, January 27, 1945.

31. Clyde Haney to Richard Haney, February 9, 1945.

Epilogue

1. *Janesville (Wisconsin) Gazette,* May 8, 1945.

2. Vera Haney Piddington's written notation on a *Wisconsin State Journal* clipping, August 14, 1995, next to a story commemorating the fiftieth anniversary of the surrender of Japan.

3. *Janesville (Wisconsin) Gazette,* August 15, 1945.

4. Ibid.

5. *Janesville (Wisconsin) Gazette,* August 22, 1945.

6. *Janesville (Wisconsin) Daily Gazette,* November 23 and December 21, 1945.

7. American Battle Monuments Commission (ABMC), "World War II Commemorative Program" (Washington, DC, ABMC, 1995), p. 12; ABMC, "American Memorials and Overseas Military Cemeteries" (Washington, DC, ABMC, 1970).

8. George C. Marshall, "Our War Memorials Abroad: A Faith Kept," *National Geographic Magazine,* June 1957, p. 731.

9. Pyle, *Here Is Your War,* p. 304.

10. Virginia (Gates) Munns, Tucson, AZ, to Richard C. Haney, March 2, 1992.

11. Ambrose, *The Victors,* p. 351.

12. The names of 188 Rock County men killed in action are on the Rock County Veterans' Memorial at the Rock County Airport between Janesville and Beloit. One hundred seventeen additional Rock County men were listed in the *Janesville Daily*

Gazette on January 2, 1946, as having been killed in World War II. Another seven were not included in either of the listings but are named in Dale Dopkins's *The Janesville 99* (Janesville, WI: Dale Dopkins, 1981). The total number of Rock County men who died in World War II is at least 302, counting the combined listings of the Rock County Veterans' Memorial, the *Janesville Daily Gazette* (January 2, 1946), and the Dopkins account. The very observant *Janesville Gazette* writer Michael Du Pre (Du Pre, *A Century of Stories,* pp. 78–79) noted the incompleteness of some of the listings. The Rock County Veterans' Memorial also lists the names of seventy-five Rock County men who were killed in World War I, thirty-two in the Korean War, and forty-three in the Vietnam War. Total: 452.

Appendix

1. Mom said that she heard Dad use a swear word only once–when he had to change a flat tire in the rain. His cursing here in connection with cracking his forehead with his rifle butt is indicative of his level of frustration.

2. The then-puzzling interview was a precursor to Dad's being assigned to Intelligence Reconnaissance and later being asked to volunteer for Officer Candidate School.

3. Mom was about to start her job at the *Janesville Gazette* to support us while Dad's civilian-life income was suspended.

4. Mom wrote on the envelope, "This letter is important to me." The reason is obvious: Dad's love for us and reassurance to her as he is about to go overseas are both heartfelt and pointed. Once Dad's orders were for overseas duty, he was no longer permitted to reveal his location or activities, and all mail addressed to him was sent in care of the New York City Postmaster to be funneled through the Army Post Office, New York.

5. This was the first message from Dad in which he slipped coded messages past the censor. References to a craving for liver and to Grandpa's nonexistent swimming pool let Mom know that his immediate destination was Liverpool, England. They had agreed that any mention of a nonexistent "Uncle Mike" would mean he was headed to Europe.

6. Once in England, Dad volunteered for the Airborne. Mom knew that the army defined airborne as "hazardous duty," so to avoid causing her undue worry Dad was upbeat and nonchalant in breaking the news.

7. In referring to "Mike" in this letter, Dad really meant himself. Censorship would not allow him to tell of his own location, but he could reveal that "Mike" and "Ted" had been stationed near Oxford. Just in case that had been censored, he also wrote about "Marlborough" cigarettes (Mom did not smoke) to tell Mom that he was stationed near Marlborough, England.

8. Dad was in the thick of combat in the Battle of the Bulge when he wrote this letter. The next day he began a weeklong hospital stay to recover from the injuries that earned him his first Purple Heart. During the first days of the Bulge, some units of the 17th Airborne Division suffered 70 percent casualties.

9. Writing from an army field hospital in Belgium, Dad was concerned that the Christmas presents he sent Mom and me from England had arrived safely. While in England, he had paid an Italian prisoner of war to make a ring for me out of melted-down Italian coins. Mom's bracelet, Dad's silver airborne wings, and my ring arrived a few days later.

10. Mom took this letter to Rock County Red Cross Director Mary Kamps, who agreed that Dad was revealing by his wristwatch remarks that he had been taken prisoner of war but managed to escape. Arrival of photos of Mom and me obviously warmed Dad's heart during the weeks of harsh winter combat.

11. This coded letter revealed that Dad was six or seven miles from Chalons-sur-Marne, France. The message is in the first letters of the words addressed to "Dad."

12. This was the first of several letters that came back to Mom stamped "Deceased: Return to Sender." She had written this letter on February 28, and it had not reached him by the time of his death on March 24. Fortunately, Mom received the "regret to inform" telegram before any of the letters came back.

13. Dad's remark that "Practically the same thing happened to us that you wrote but it is nothing to talk about. It's a messy business–thats all I care to say," is in response to an earlier reference Mom made to the Malmedy Massacre in the Battle of the Bulge, where German SS troops murdered several dozen American prisoners of war by machine-gunning them to death in an open field. It confirmed Mom's belief that Dad had been taken prisoner of war but escaped.

14. Dad's last letter included the message "Airborne Mission Soon" encoded in the first letters of words addressed to "Dad." He was killed in the air drop over the Rhine River five days later.

Index